NEW DIRECTIONS IN KNITTING

Edited by Jeanne Stauffer
Exclusively using Plymouth yarns

HOUSE of
WHITE
BIRCHES

PUBLISHERS
SINCE 1947

New Directions in Knitting

Editor: Jeanne Stauffer
Associate Editors: Rachelle Haughn, Dianne Schmidt
Book and Cover Design: Jessi Butler

Pattern Editors: E.J. Slayton, Diane Zangl
Design Associate: Vicki Blizzard
Copy Editors: Nicki Lehman, Mary Martin

Photography: Scott Campbell, Andy Burnfield
Photography Assistant: Linda Quinlan
Production Artist: Edith Teegarden
Production Assistants: Janet Bowers, Marj Morgan
Traffic Coordinator: Sandra Beres
Technical Artists: Liz Morgan, Mitch Moss, Travis Spangler, Chad Summers

Publishers: Carl H. Muselman, Arthur K. Muselman
Chief Executive Officer: John Robinson
Publishing Marketing Director: David McKee
Book Marketing Manager: Craig Scott
Editorial Director: Vivian Rothe
Publishing Services Director: Brenda R. Wendling
Publishing Services Manager: Brenda Gallmeyer

Printed in the United States of America
First Printing: 2003
Library of Congress Number: 2001097995
ISBN: 1-882138-96-1

Retail outlet owners and resellers: For additional copies of this book call (800) 772-6643.

Get ready for some fun! Try these unusual knitting techniques for stitching sweaters. Start at one cuff and knit to the other cuff. Or start at the shoulders and knit down to the waist. Or knit diagonally from corner to corner. Or knit a cable that goes from cuff to cuff and pick up stitches to knit up and down along the cable. I could go on and list more ways you can knit in new directions, but I'll let you discover them for yourself when you try out the great sweater designs in this book.

If you have only made sweaters starting at the waist and knitting to the shoulders, you will be delighted with this new way of looking at the process of knitting. You'll find that many sweaters that are knit from side to side have slimming vertical lines. Those that are knit from the top down can be lengthened when a child shoots up overnight. In fact, one of my designer friends always makes oversized sweaters for her children, so they can wear them for years and years. You can spend more time knitting and less time sewing seams with many of these new directions in knitting.

In this collection, you'll find designs for the entire family, for every season of the year and for any occasion. We know that some knitters like cardigans and others pullovers, so we have some of each. Teenagers have their own style, but there are sweaters and tops that will please them as well. Whatever your style, you can knit it in a new direction!

Warm regards,

Jeanne Stauffer

Welcome

Weekend in the Country

A Beach Holiday

A Mountain Sojourn

Life in the City

Contents

Weekend in the Country

Indigo Cotton Vest

Design by Katharine Hunt

The combination of a zigzag color change, garter stitch and cotton yarn creates a classic vest.

Skill Level
Intermediate***

Size
Woman's small (medium, large) Instructions are given for smallest size, with larger sizes in parentheses. When only 1 number is given, it applies to all sizes.

Finished Measurements
Chest: 38 (42, 46) inches

Length: 19½ (20½, 21½) inches

Materials
- Plymouth Blu Jeans DK weight 100 percent indigo-dyed cotton yarn (118 yds/50g per skein): 6 (7, 8) skeins natural #1, 2 skeins medium blue #3
- Size 3 (3.25mm) straight and circular needles
- Size 6 (4mm) needles or size needed to obtain gauge
- Cable needle
- Tapestry needle
- 6 (6, 7) ⅝-inch buttons

Gauge
27 sts = 4 inches/10cm in Slip Stitch Zigzag pat with larger needles

26 sts = 4 inches/10cm in garter st with smaller needles

To save time, take time to check gauge.

Pattern Notes
Body of vest is worked sideways in 1 piece, in Sl St Zigzag pat. Bodice is picked up along top edge of body, and worked vertically in garter st. Bands are picked up and worked in garter st. (see Fig. 1)

Sl all sts purlwise.

Carry color not in use up side of work, catching it with working color.

When picking up sts along edge of SSZ body, avoid working into yarn carried up side of work.

Where cn is called for, you may find it faster simply to drop the st and pick it up in the appropriate position, instead of using cn. If desired, use cn for first few reps, to familiarize yourself with pat, then try it without.

Special Abbreviations
C3L (cable 3 left): Sl 1 to cn, hold in front, k2, k1 from cn.

C3R (cable 3 right): Sl next 2 sts to cn and hold in back, k1, k2 from cn.

Pattern Stitches
Sl St Zigzag (SSZ): (multiple of 4 sts + 1)

Row 1 (RS): With blue, k5, *sl 1, k3, rep from * across.

Row 2: With blue, *p3, sl 1, rep from * to last 5 sts, p5.

Row 3: With natural, k3, *C3R, k1, rep from * to last 2 sts, k2.

Row 4: With natural, purl across.

Row 5: With blue, k1, *sl 1, k3, rep from * across.

Row 6: With blue, *p3, sl 1, rep from * to last st, p1.

Row 7: With natural, k1, *C3L, k1, rep from * across.

Row 8: With natural, purl across.

Rep Rows 1–8 for pat.

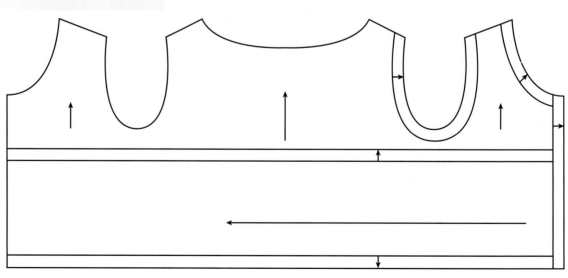

FIG. 1
Arrows show direction of knitting

Sl St Trim (SST)

Row 1 (RS): With blue, k2, sl 1 wyib,*k3, sl 1 wyib, rep from * to last 2 sts, k2.

Row 2 (WS): With blue, k2, sl 1 wyif, *k3, sl 1 wyif, rep from * to last 2 sts, k2.

Body

With natural and larger needles, cast on 61 (65, 69) sts, p 1 row.

Rows 1 and 2 (RS): Attach blue and work Rows 1 and 2 of SSZ.

Change to natural and continue in SSZ, changing colors as noted, until work measures 37 (41, 45) inches from beg, ending with Row 8 of pat.

With natural, k 1 row, then bind off purlwise on WS.

Bottom Border

With circular needle and natural, RS facing, pick up and k 237 (265, 289) sts along bottom edge of body. K 1 row (WS). With blue, work 2 rows SST. With natural, work 5 rows garter st. Bind off knitwise on WS.

Yoke

Rep border on top edge of body, ending with 5 rows of garter st. Do not bind off.

Continue in garter st until work measures 10½ (11, 11½)

inches from bottom edge, ending with a WS row.

Shape armholes

In garter st, work 48 (54, 60) sts, bind off 20 (21, 21) sts, work 101 (115, 127) sts, bind off 20 (22, 22) sts, work 48 (54, 60) sts.

Attach new balls at beg of back and 2nd front and work all pieces at same time, shaping armholes as follows: dec 1 st at each armhole edge [every row] 5 times, [every RS row] 5 times, then [every other RS row] 3 times.

Work even until piece measures 5¼ (5½, 5¾) inches from armhole bind off, ending with a WS row.

Shape front neck

Rows 1 and 2: Working across all sts, bind off 9 (11, 13) sts at first front neck edge, dec 1 st at 2nd front neck edge.

Rows 3 and 4: Working across all sts, bind off 2 sts at first front neck edge and dec 1 st at 2nd front neck edge.

Continue to dec 1 st at both front neck edges [every row] 4 times, then every RS row until 14 (18, 22) sts remain. *At the same time,* work even on back until work measures 8¼ (8½, 9) inches from armhole bind off, ending with a WS row.

Shape back neck

Continuing to work even on fronts, work back neck shaping as follows: k26 (30, 34), bind off 23 (29, 33) sts, k26 (30, 34).

Row 1 (WS): K24 (28, 32), k2tog; attach new ball to 2nd back neck edge, ssk, k to end.

Row 2: K to last 2 sts, k2tog; bind off 2 sts at neck edge, k to end.

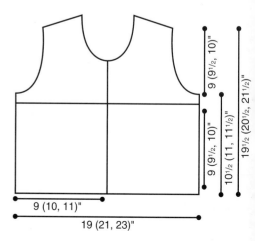

9 (9½, 10)"

9 (9½, 10)"

10½ (11, 11½)"

19½ (20½, 21½)"

9 (10, 11)"

19 (21, 23)"

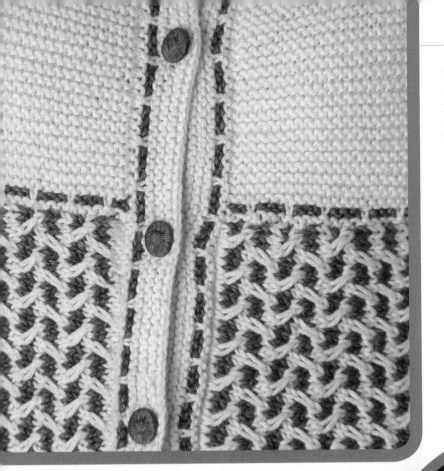

7 sts, k3. Turn, leaving last 4 sts on needle.

Row 4 (WS): With blue, skip first 4 natural sts, *k3, sl 1 wyif, rep from * to last 7 sts, k3. Turn, leaving last 4 sts on needle.

Row 5: With natural, k across all sts.

Rows 6–11: With natural, knit.

Row 12: Bind off knitwise on WS.

With pins, mark band for 6 (6, 6, 7) buttons evenly spaced, beg and ending approximately ½ inch from ends.

Buttonhole band

Work as for left band, picking up and k sts from bottom to neck edge.

On Row 7, bind off 2 sts at each buttonhole location, then cast on 2 sts above each hole on Row 8. Complete to match other band.

Sew buttons in place on button band.

Note: *Do not wet block.* ❖

Rows 3–6: Rep Row 2.

Knit, dec 1 st at each back neck edge [every row] until 14 (18, 22) sts remain.

Shape shoulders

When work measures 9 (9½, 10) inches from underarm, working across all pieces with RS facing, bind off first 7 (6, 8) sts at beg of back and left front. On next row, rep at other edge of back and right front. Rep previous 2 rows. On medium (large), rep again, binding off remaining 6 sts on each piece.

Finishing

Armhole bands

Beg at left back shoulder with circular needle and natural, RS facing, pick up and k 125 (129, 137) sts, ending at left front shoulder.

Row 1 (WS): Knit.

Rows 2 and 3: Attach blue and work SST. Cut blue.

With natural, work 5 rows garter st. Bind off knitwise on WS.

Rep on other armhole, picking up sts from right front shoulder around to right back shoulder.

Sew shoulder seams.

Neck band

Beg at right front neck edge with circular needle and natural, RS facing, pick up and k 137 (145, 153) sts around neckline, ending at left front.

Work as for sleeve bands, except dec 14 (16, 18) sts evenly on 9th row. Bind off knitwise on WS.

Button band

Row 1: With natural and circular needle, RS facing, pick up and k 105 (109, 117) sts, from neck edge to bottom of left front, working over end edges of neck band and bottom border.

Row 2: Knit.

Row 3: (RS): With blue, sl 4, *k3, sl 1 wyib, rep from * to last

Caravan Vest

Design by Diane Zangl

This warm, rustic garment features a unique pattern in which the stitches lay perpendicular to the direction of the work. The patterned fabric is created by picking up stitches, turning, and immediately binding them off.

Skill Level

Advanced****

Size

Adult's small (medium, large)
Instructions are given for smallest size, with larger sizes in parentheses. When only 1 number is given, it applies to all sizes.

Finished Measurements

Chest: 38 (44, 48) inches

Side to underarm: 10 (10½, 11) inches

Armhole depth: 8½ (9½, 10) inches

Materials

- Plymouth Galway worsted weight 100 percent wool yarn (210 yds/ 100g per skein): 4 (4, 5) skeins gray #702 (MC), 1 skein each burgundy #710 and blue #732
- Size 6 (4mm) double-pointed needles (2 only)
- Size 7 (4.5mm) needles or size needed to obtain gauge
- Stitch markers
- Size G/6 (4mm) crochet hook
- 6 (⅞-inch) buttons, New Age #35717 from JHB International Inc.

Gauge

20 sts and 14 rows = 4 inches/10cm in Bound-Off Braid pat

To save time, take time to check gauge.

Pattern Notes

Vest begins at center back and is worked toward center front. Second half is a mirror-image of first. Each row consists of two parts, the picked-up half of the row and the bound-off half.

Bound-off sts will tip forward and lay on face of fabric in a horizontal position. Make sure to keep st count constant when picking up sts; it is very easy to miss the last st.

When working color pat, chart indicates which color to pick up. Bind off in color pat.

Work I-cord around all openings.

Chart does not have to be reversed for 2nd half of vest.

Pattern Stitch

BOB (bound-off braid)

All rows (right half of vest): With RS facing, pick up and k 1 st in each p bump of previous row (see Fig. 1), turn, bind off purlwise.

All rows (left half of vest): With WS facing, pick up and p 1 st in each p bump of previous row (see Fig. 2), turn, bind off knitwise.

Vest

Right Half

Beg at center back with MC, cast on 93 (99, 105) sts. Bind off all sts.

Work even in BOB for 3 rows.

Referring to chart, work in color pat for 8 rows.

Work in MC only until vest measures 6¾ (7¼, 7¾) inches. Mark last row.

Shape underarm

Working on 50 (53, 55) sts only and leaving remaining sts unworked, work even for 5½ (7½, 8½) inches above marker. Mark last row.

Next row: Pick up and k 1 st in each st of last row, cast on 43 (46, 50) sts, turn, bind off all sts purlwise.

Work even in established pat on 93 (99, 105) sts until vest measures 3¼ (3½, 4) inches above last marker.

Shape front

Next row: Referring to chart, beg color pat, *at the same time,* pick up and k to last 3 (3, 7) sts, turn, bind off.

[Work 3 sts less on each following row] 7 times more, [then 2 sts less on each row] 8 (9, 9) times. (53, 57, 59 sts before binding off final row)

Left Half

With WS facing pick up and p 1 st in each cast-on st of right half (93, 99,

105 sts), turn, bind off knitwise.

Work left half as for right, reversing shaping and substituting left-worked BOB.

Sew shoulder seams.

I-Cord Edging

Armhole

Beg at center of underarm using dpn, pick up a section of sts at a ratio of 4 sts for every 5 sts or rows.

With 2nd dpn and MC, cast on 3 sts. *Sl sts back to LH needle, k2, ssk. Rep from * until all picked-up sts have been worked. Continue to pick up additional sections of sts and work around entire armhole. Cut yarn, leaving a 12-inch end. Sew final sts to cast-on sts.

Body

Beg at center back neck, work I-cord around entire body opening as for armholes.

Finishing

Mark each front edge for 3 buttons evenly spaced below neck shaping.

Ties

Make 6

Attach MC to marked st. Using crochet hook, ch 25, turn, work 1 sl st in each st of ch. Fasten off.

Sew button over tie. ❖

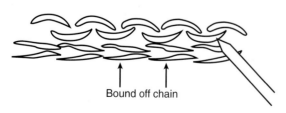

FIG. 1
Pick up in k: Tip work forward slightly, pick up and k in top bar behind bound-off ch.

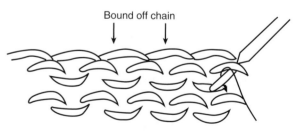

FIG. 2
Pick up in p: Insert needle under top bar of st, wrap yarn around needle as if to p, pull loop through st.

VEST
RIGHT HALF

CENTER BACK

8½ (9½, 10)"   10 (10½, 11)"

3½ (3¾, 3¾)"

3¼ (3½, 4)"

5½ (7½, 8½)"

3¼ (3½, 4)"

3½ (3¾, 3¾)"

19 (22, 24)"

18½ (20, 21)"

COLOR KEY
- Gray
- Burgundy
- Blue

8
7
6
5
6
3
2
1

COLOR CHART

Royal Ashanti Jacket

Design by Barbara Venishnick

Just like the famous Kente cloth of the Ashanti people, this jacket is made in narrow strips that are joined together to form a wide fabric. To replicate the alternating warp- and weft-faced blocks of the woven cloth, the designer used garter stitch stripes in blocks that are knit from the bottom up and from side to side alternately. When they are joined together, care should be taken to place vertical blocks next to horizontal blocks to further the effect.

Skill Level

Intermediate***

Size

Woman's small/medium (large/ extra-large) Instructions are given for smaller size, with larger size in parentheses. When only 1 number is given, it applies to both sizes.

Finished Measurements

Chest: 47 (55) inches
Length: 23½ (27½) inches

Materials

- Plymouth Encore worsted weight 75 percent acrylic/25 percent wool yarn (200 yds/100g per ball): 3 (4) balls each taupe #1204 (A), camel #1203 (C)
- Plymouth Encore Colorspun worsted weight 75 percent acrylic/25 percent wool yarn (200 yds/100g per ball): 3 (4) balls golden tweed #7301 (B)
- Size 8 (5mm) straight and 40-inch circular needles or size needed to obtain gauge
- Size F/5 (3.75mm) crochet hook
- Tapestry needle

Gauge

16 sts and 36 rows = 4 inches/10cm in garter st with larger needles

To save time, take time to check gauge.

Pattern Note

The number of rows in each block must be exactly twice the number of

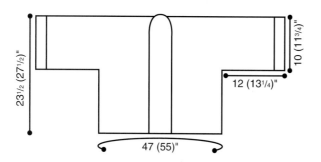

23½ (27½)"
10 (11¾)"
12 (13¼)"
47 (55)"

sts so they can fit together precisely. The stripe pattern uses three colors, so each block must be a multiple of three in both sts and rows. Each of these factors restricts the ability to vary the size of the final piece. The pattern is written in two sizes, small/medium and large/extra-large. Further variation can be achieved by changing the gauge slightly.

Special Technique

Cable cast on: *Insert RH needle between first and 2nd st on LH needle and draw up a loop. Place loop on LH needle creating a new first st. Rep from * until desired number of sts have been added.

Strip

Square 1 (used at beg of strip only)

With A, cast on 15 (18) sts.

Rows 1–10: With A, k1 tbl, k13 (16), sl 1 knitwise wyif.

Rows 11–20: With B, rep Rows 1–10.

Rows 21–29: With C, rep Rows 1–9.

Row 30 (WS): With C, bind off all sts, leaving last loop on needle. Do not cut yarn.

Square 2

Hold Square 1 with WS facing. Using last loop of bound-off edge as first st, pick up and p 14 (17) more sts, 1 in each edge st along side of Square 1, turn. (15, 18 sts)

Rows 1–10: With C, k1 tbl, k13 (16), sl 1 knitwise wyif.

Rows 11–20: With B, rep Rows 1–10.

Rows 21–30: With A, rep Rows 1–10. Leave all sts on needle and yarn still attached.

Square 3

With RS facing, using A, cable cast on 15 (18) sts.

Row 1: With A, k1 tbl, k13 (16), sl 1 knitwise wyib, k1, psso, turn.

Row 2: With A, k14 (17), sl 1 knitwise wyif.

Rows 3–10: Rep Rows 1 and 2.

Rows 11–20: With B, rep Rows 1–10.

Rows 21–29: With C, rep Rows 1–9.

Row 30: With C, bind off all sts, leaving last loop on needle. Do not cut yarn.

Rep Squares 2 and 3 alternately until desired number of squares is completed. At end of final square, bind off all sts.

Jacket Body

Make 6 strips of 14 squares each.

Sleeves

Make 3 strips of 6 squares for each sleeve, a total 6 strips of 6 squares each.

Center Back Strip

(beg in middle of Square 2)

With B, cast on 15 (18) sts.

Rows 1–10: Work Rows 11–20 of Square 2.

Rows 11–20: Work Rows 21–30 of Square 2.

Continue as for regular strips, alternating Squares 3 and 2 until 6 full squares are made after first partial square.

Assemble Strips

Referring to Fig. 1 for placement, hold 2 long strips tog lengthwise, RS tog, with cast on edge of Square 1 next to side edge of Square 2. With C and crochet hook, work 1 sc in each st or ridge through both layers along entire length of strip, taking care to line up corners.

Note: *Place hook through edge st of 1 layer and either bound off or cast on st of other layer.*

Unfold these 2 strips. Join a 3rd long strip, again alternating position of first square, and crochet tog as before. Unfold.

Attach center back strip in same manner, making sure that half square is placed at back neck. Attach remaining long strips for body. Add shorter sleeve strips, positioned as indicated on Fig. 1.

I-Cord Trim

Hold jacket with RS facing. Beg at lower right center edge, with B and long circular needle, pick up and k 1

COLOR KEY
■ Taupe (A)
□ Golden tweed (B)
▨ Camel (C)

FIG. 1

st in each ridge, cast on or bound off st along right side, across back neck and down left side, then cast on 4 more sts using twisted loop cast-on. Turn. *K3, k next st tog with 1 picked up st, sl 4 sts back to left needle, pull yarn across back of work. Rep from * until all picked up sts are worked. Bind off remaining 4 sts.

Front Band

Hold work with RS facing as for I-cord trim. Hold trim down and with A and long circular needle, pick up and k 1 st in each of same places as for I-cord. Turn. Knit 9 rows, ending with a WS row.

With C, knit 1 row, then, bind off all sts knitwise on WS.

Sleeve Cuff

Work I-cord and band as for front.

Finishing

Fold jacket inside out. With C and crochet hook, join side seams and underarm seams using same method as for joining strips. Turn RS out and block lightly. ❖

Top-Down Pullover

Design by Edie Eckman

A full yoke trimmed with lace is a delight to knit from the top down.

Skill Level

Intermediate***

Size

Woman's small (medium, large)
Instructions are given for smallest size, with larger sizes in parentheses. When only 1 number is given, it applies to all sizes.

Finished Measurements

Chest: 39 (43, 47) inches
Length: 23¾ (25¼, 26¾) inches

Materials

- Plymouth Galway worsted weight 100 percent wool yarn (210 yds/ 100g per skein): 6 (7, 8) balls raspberry #19
- Size 8 (5mm) double-pointed, 16- and 24-inch circular needles or size needed to obtain gauge
- Stitch markers
- Tapestry needle

Gauge

20 sts and 24 rows = 4 inches/10cm in St st

To save time, take time to check gauge.

Special Abbreviation

Inc 1: Knit or purl into top of purl "bump" below next st on RH needle.

Body

With 16-inch needle, cast on 84 (90, 96) sts, pm at beg of rnd and join without twisting.

Rnd 1: *K3, p3, rep from * around.

Rep Rnd 1 until piece measures 2 inches. Change to longer circular needle as needed.

Yoke

Rnd 1: *K2, k1 in front and back of next st, [p1 in front and back of next st] 3 times, rep from * around. (140, 150, 160 sts)

Rnds 2–6: *K3, p7, rep from * around.

Rnd 7: K2, *yo, ssk, p5, k2tog, yo, k1, rep from *, end p5, remove marker, k2tog, yo, replace marker.

Rnd 8: *K3, p5, k2, rep from * around.

Rnd 9: K2, *yo, ssk, p3, k2tog, yo, k3, rep from *, end last rep k1.

Rnd 10: K4, *p3, k7, rep from *, end k3.

Rnd 11: K1, *[yo, ssk] twice, p1, [k2tog, yo] twice, k1, rep from *, end last rep k0.

Rnd 12: K5, *p1, k9, rep from *, end last rep k4.

Rnd 13: K2, *yo, ssk, yo, sl 1, k2tog, psso, yo, k2tog, yo, k3, end last rep k1.

Rnds 14, 16 and 18: Knit.

Rnd 15: K3, *yo, ssk, k1, k2tog, yo, k5, rep from *, end last rep k2.

Rnd 17: K4, *yo, sl 1, k2tog, psso, yo, k7, rep from *, end last rep k3.

Rnd 19: K2, *k3, [k1, p1, k1, p1, k1] in next st, pass 2nd, 3rd, 4th and 5th sts on RH needle over first st, k6, rep from * around, end last rep k4.

Rnd 20: Knit, k in back of each bobble st.

Inc rnd small only: *[K2, inc 1] twice, k3, inc 1, rep from *, end k2. (200 sts)

Inc rnd medium (large) only: *K2, inc 1, rep from *. (225, 240 sts)

Work even in St st until piece measures 4¾ (5¼, 5¾) inches from beg of yoke.

Inc rnd small (medium) only: K1, *inc 1, k3, rep from *, end last rep k4 (2). (266, 300 sts)

Inc rnd large only: K1, *[inc 1, k3] 4 times, [inc 1, k2] twice, rep from *, end last rep k1. (330 sts)

Work even until piece measures 9¼ (10¼, 11¼) inches from beg of yoke.

Divide for underarm

K 82 (91, 101) sts for back, sl next 51 (59, 64) sts onto waste yarn for left sleeve, cast on 16 (17, 18) sts, k 82 (91, 101) sts for front, sl remaining 51 (59, 64) sts onto waste yarn for right sleeve, cast on 16 (17, 18) sts.

Work even in St st on 196 (216, 238) body sts until sweater measures 12½ (13, 13½) inches from underarm, or 2 inches less than desired length. Dec 10 (12, 10) sts evenly on next rnd.

Work in k3, p3 ribbing for 2 inches. Bind off in pat.

Sleeves

Sl 51 (59, 64) sts from right sleeve holder onto smaller circular needle, cast on 17 (17, 18) sts. Place marker at center underarm.

Work even in St st on 67 (76, 82) sts for 1½ (1½, 1½) inches, then dec 1 st on each side of marker [every 7th rnd] 6 (0, 0) times, [every 6th rnd] 7 (14, 8) times, and [every 5th rnd] 0 (0, 8) times. (42, 48, 50 sts)

Work even until sleeve measures 15½ (15½, 16) inches from underarm. Dec 6 (6, 8) sts evenly on next rnd. Work k3, p3 rib as for body. Bind off in pat. Work 2nd sleeve to match.

Finishing

Weave underarm sts tog. ❖

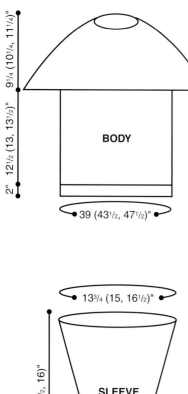

BODY

9¼ (10¼, 11¼)"

12½ (13, 13½)"

2"

39 (43½, 47½)"

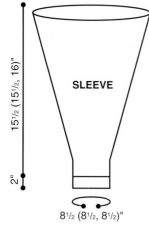

SLEEVE

13¾ (15, 16½)"

15½ (15½, 16)"

2"

8½ (8½, 8½)"

Country Fiesta

Design by Nazanin S. Fard

*Worked entirely in the round, there are no side or sleeve seams
for this top-down sweater accented with a stylish boat neck.*

Skill Level
Intermediate***

Size
Woman's small (size 10)

Finished Measurements
Chest: 38 inches

Length: 25 inches

Sleeve length: 20 inches

Materials
- Plymouth Filati Bertagna Imperiale Super Kid Mohair, worsted weight 80 percent mohair/20 percent polyamide yarn (109 yds/25g per skein): 10 skeins ivory #4102 (MC), 2 skeins fiesta #4185 (CC)
- Size 5 (3.75mm) double-pointed (optional for cuff) and circular needle
- Size 6 (4mm) circular needles or size needed to obtain gauge
- Stitch holder
- Stitch marker
- Tapestry needle
- Size E/4 (3.5mm) crochet hook

Gauge
19 sts and 26 rows = 4 inches/10cm in St st with larger needles

To save time, take time to check gauge.

Back
With larger needles, cast on 101 sts. Work 10 rows of St st.

Referring to Charts A and B, work Rows 1–3 of Pat A, then Rows 1–15 o[f] Pat B. *Work Rows 1–3 of Pat A, with MC, work 12 rows of St st, rep from * until piece measures 9½ inches. Leave all sts on holder.

Front
Work to match back, leaving sts on needle.

Body
Join front and back and work in rnds, pm at beg of rnd. Work even in established pat until piece measures 23 inches, then change to smaller needles and work k 1, p1 ribbing for 2 inches. Bind off all sts in pat.

Sleeve
Sew shoulder seams (approximately 4 inches on each side of neck opening).

Beg at underarm, pick up and k 101 sts around armhole, pm at beg of rnd.

Work 6 rnds of St st then switch to pat as for body, dec 2 sts at underarm [every 15 rnds] 7 times. (87 sts remaining at cuff)

Dec 27 sts evenly on next rnd. With smaller dpn, work in k1, p1 ribbing for 1½ inches. Bind off in pat.

Finishing

With crochet hook and CC, work 1 rnd of sc around neck opening, then work 1 rnd of reverse sc (crab st). Fasten off.

Block sweater to size. ❖

COLOR KEY
☐ MC
☒ CC

Rep
CHART A

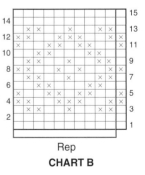

Rep
CHART B

Point-to-Point Blouse

Design by Nazanin S. Fard

This charming bicolor blouse is worked from one point on the side to the shoulder on the other. The design has stripes of stockinette stitch, which creates a stunning look. Working the sleeves in different colors adds to the whimsical look of the blouse. The bottom-edge ribbing and neck trim continue the bicolor theme.

Skill Level

Intermediate***

Size

Woman's small (size 10)

Finished Measurements

Chest: 38 inches

Length: 22 inches

Sleeve length: 17 inches

Materials

- Plymouth Fantasy Naturale worsted weight 100 percent mercerized cotton yarn (140 yds/100g per skein): 4 skeins rose #3706 (MC), 3 skeins ecru #8176 (CC)
- Tapestry needle
- Size 6 (4mm) needles
- Size 8 (5mm) needles or size needed to obtain gauge
- Size G/6 (4mm) crochet hook

Gauge:

14 sts and 26 rows = 4 inches/10cm in St st with larger needles

To save time, take time to check gauge.

Pattern Notes

Do not cut yarn between stripes, carry colors loosely along edge.

Front and back of sweater require heavy blocking.

Front

Beg at shoulder with larger needles and MC, cast on 3 sts.

Row 1: Knit.

Row 2 and all WS rows: Purl.

Row 3: With CC, k in front and back of first st, k to last st, k in front and back of last st.

Row 5: With MC, rep Row 3.

Continue to work in pat, alternating colors every other row until end of Row 178. (91 sts)

Start decreasing as follows:

Row 179: Ssk, k to last 2 sts, k2tog.

Row 180: Purl.

Rep Rows 179 and 180, alternating colors as before until 3 sts remain. Bind off. Do not cut yarn.

Bottom border

With smaller needles and MC, WS facing, pick up and p 90 sts across lower edge. Work in k 1, p 1 ribbing for 15 rows, alternating colors every other row. Bind off in pat.

Back

Work same as front.

Sleeves

Note: Work 1 sleeve in each color.

With smaller needles, cast on 40 sts. Work k 1, p1 ribbing for 8 rows.

Change to larger needles, inc 10 sts evenly in first row. (50 sts)

Work in St st, inc 1 st on each side [every 6th row] 14 times. (78 sts)

Work even until sleeve measures 17 inches. Bind off all sts.

Finishing

Block front, back and sleeves separately. Sew shoulder seams, leaving approximately 11 inches open for neck.

Twisted edging

Rnd 1: With crochet hook and CC, attach yarn to corner of neckline, *sc, ch 1, skip next st, rep from * around. Fasten off.

Rnd 2: With MC, attach yarn to same corner as Rnd 1, sc in same st, *ch 1, remove hook from loop, insert hook under ch 1 st of previous row, ch 1, rep from * around. Fasten off.

Pm 9 inches down from shoulder seam on each side. Sew sleeves to body between markers. Sew sleeve and body seams. ❖

Periwinkle Panels

Design by Barbara Venishnick

Modular construction allows this complex, yet beautiful sweater to be knit together at your own pace.

Skill Level
Advanced****

Size
Woman's small (medium, large) Instructions are given for smallest size, with larger sizes in parentheses. When only 1 number is given, it applies to all sizes.

Finished Measurements
Chest: 40 (44, 48) inches
Length: 22 (23, 24) inches

Materials
- Plymouth Indiecita worsted weight 100 percent Peruvian alpaca yarn (102 yds/50g per ball): 16 (17, 18) balls purple #1720
- Size 5 (3.75mm) straight, 20- and 29-inch circular needles or size needed to obtain gauge
- Cable needle
- Stitch markers
- Stitch holders
- Tapestry needle

Gauge
20 sts and 28 rows = 4 inches/10cm in St st

To save time, take time to check gauge.

Special Abbreviation
M1 (make 1): Lift running thread between st just knit and next st, place on left needle, k 1 in back.

Pattern Note
Sweater is worked in following order:

1. Work front and back entrelac panels.

2. Join front and back panels, work funnel collar in rnds.

3. Make 2 cable bands, sew on each side of center panels.

4. Pick up and k side body along edge of cable bands, work to side seam. Sleeves are continued to cuff after binding off body sts. Join body and sleeve underarm seams.

5. Pick up and k picot hem around lower edge.

Center Panel
With 2 straight needles held tog, cast on 32 sts for all sizes. Withdraw 1 needle, leaving loosely cast on sts on other needle.

Note: This special cast on is used only for entrelac section. Entrelac panel has a lot of sideways stretch and a loose cast on prevents bottom edge from pulling in.

Row 1 (WS base triangles): *P2, turn, k2, turn, p3, turn, k3, turn, p4, leave these sts on RH needle (1 triangle completed). Rep from * over next 7 groups of 4 sts, a total of 8 base triangles.

Row 2 (RS rectangles): Beg row with a side triangle, k2, turn, p2, turn, k1, M1, k2tog, turn, p3, turn, k1, M1, k1, k2tog, do not turn, leave side triangle on RH needle. Work RS rectangle, pick up and k 4 sts along side of first base triangle, *[turn, p4, turn, k3, k2tog] 4 times, do not turn (RS rectangle completed). Pick up and k 4 sts along side of next base triangle and rep from *. Work a total of 7 RS rectangles. End row with a side triangle, pick up and k 4 sts along side of last base triangle, turn, p4, turn, k2, k2tog, turn, p3, turn, k1, k2tog, turn, p2, turn, k2tog, turn.

Row 3 (WS rectangles, no triangles are needed on this row): P 1 st remaining from last side triangle of previous row, pick up and p 3 sts along side of this triangle, *[turn, k4, turn, p3, p2tog] 4 times, do not turn (WS rectangle completed). Pick up and p 4 sts along side of first

rectangle of row below and rep from * until 8 WS rectangles are completed. [Rep Rows 2 and 3] 17 (18, 19) more times. Cut yarn and place all sts on 20-inch circular needle.

Work 2nd entrelac panel in same way. At end of last row of WS rectangles, do not cut yarn. With RS facing sl sts of first panel to left end of circular needle, sl sts of 2nd panel onto beg of needle so it will be worked first. Turn work.

Join panels for funnel neck
Note: When working entrelac in rnds, triangles are only needed to fill in top on last rnd.

Rnd 1: With attached yarn, WS facing, pick up and p 4 sts along edge of last rectangle of first panel, [turn, k3, k2tog (1 st of new rectangle with 1 st of 2nd panel), p4] 3 times, turn, k3, k2tog, do not turn. *Pick up and k 4 sts along side of next rectangle of first panel and complete a RS rectangle as above. Rep from * around, joining other edges of panels, until 16 RS rectangles are completed.

Rnd 2: Pick up and k 4 sts along side of next rectangle, turn. Turn work inside out. Work a WS rectangle, p3, p2tog, [turn, k4, turn, p3, p2tog] 3 times, do not turn. *Pick up and p 4 sts along side of next rectangle, and complete a WS rectangle as above, rep from * until 16 WS rectangles are completed.

Rnd 3: Pick up and p 4 sts along side of next rectangle, turn. Turn work RS out and work a round of RS rectangles as Rnd 1.

Rnds 4–7: [Rep Rnds 2 and 3] twice. (4 rnds of RS rectangles, 3 rnds of WS rectangles)

Pick up and k 4 sts along side of next rectangle, turn. Turn work inside out

Top triangles
*P3, p2tog, turn, k3, turn, sl 1, p1,

2tog, turn, k2, turn, sl 1, p2tog, [t]urn, k1, turn, p2tog, leave 4 sts on [r]ight needle. Pick up and p 4 sts [a]long side of next rectangle, turn, [k]4, turn. Rep from * until 16 top [t]riangles are made, ending with 64 [s]ts on needle.

[P]icot bind off

[W]ith WS facing, bind off 2 sts knit-[w]ise, *sl last st back to left needle, [c]able cast on 2 sts, bind off 4 sts, [r]ep from * around. Fasten off last st. [T]urn work RS out, lay aside.

[B]raided Cable Band

[M]ake 2

[C]ast on 18 sts.

[R]ow 1 and all WS rows: P2, k1, p12, [k]1, p2.

[R]ow 2: K1, sl 1, p1, k12, p1, sl 1, k1.

[R]ow 4: K1, sl 1, sl 4 sts to cn, hold in [f]ront, k4, k4 from cn, k4, p1, sl 1, k1.

[R]ow 6: Rep Row 2.

[R]ow 8: K1, sl 1, p1, k4, sl 4 sts to cn, hold in back, k4, k4 from cn, p1, sl 1, k1.

Rep [Rows 1–8] 44 (46, 48) times. Work Rows 1 and 2 once more. Bind off all sts.

Note: *To mirror-image cables on each side of center, beg 2nd cable band with Row 5 and work same number of reps as first band. End by working Rows 5 and 6 once more.*

Join cable bands to center panels

Fold cable bands in half and mark center for top of shoulders. Pin bands to each side of center panel, matching center top of shoulder to bottom of neck where front and back join. Sew in place.

Side & Sleeve

With long circular needle and RS facing, pick up and k 110 (115, 120) sts along side of cable band between bottom edge and top of shoulder, pm. Pick up and k same number of sts along side of cable band from top of shoulder down to bottom. (220, 230, 240 sts)

Turn and purl 1 row.

Shape shoulder

Row 1: K to within 3 sts of marker, k2tog, k1, sl marker, k1, ssk, k to end of row.

Rows 2–4: Work in St st.

Rep Rows 1–4 for a total of 6 dec rows, then continue to work even on 208 (218, 228) sts until side measures 4 (5, 6) inches from picked up edge, ending with a WS row. Place first and last 54 (59, 64) sts on holders for side seam.

Sleeves

Work in St st on remaining 100 sts. Dec 1 st at each side [every 4th row] 24 times, then [every 6th row] 3 times. Work even on 46 sts for 6 more rows, ending with a WS row.

Picot hem

K1, *k2tog, yo, rep from * across, end k1.

P1 row, k1 row, p1 row, bind off all sts knitwise.

Rep for other side and sleeve.

Finishing

Return side seam sts to needles and weave or bind off front and back sts tog. Sew underarm seams.

Fold sleeve hems to inside along picot edge and sew in place.

Hem

Hold work upside down with RS facing. Beg at corner of center panel

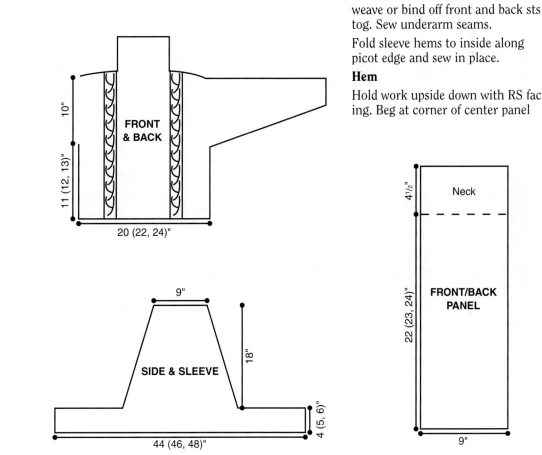

CABLE PANEL

44 (46, 48)"

1½"

FRONT & BACK

10"

11 (12, 13)"

20 (22, 24)"

SIDE & SLEEVE

9"

18"

44 (46, 48)"

4 (5, 6)"

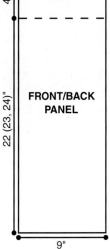

Neck

4½"

FRONT/BACK PANEL

22 (23, 24)"

9"

with longer circular needle, pick up and k 32 sts along edge of center panel, 7 sts along bottom of cable band, 39 (42, 45) sts along side section, 7 sts along cable band, 32 sts along center panel, 7 sts along cable band, 39 (42, 45) sts along side section, 7 sts along cable band, pm for beg of rnd. (170, 176, 182 sts)

P 1 rnd, k 1 rnd.

Next rnd: *P2tog, yo, rep from * around.

K 3 rnds. Bind off knitwise.

Fold hem to inside along picot edge and sew in place. ❖

Halloween Fun Sweater

Design by Kathy Sasser

The ghosts and goblins of Halloween will think that you are really into the "spirit" of things with this bright and festive sweater!

Skill Level

Advanced****

Size

Woman's small (medium, large) Instructions are given for smallest size, with larger sizes in parentheses. When only 1 number is given, it applies to all sizes.

Finished Measurements

Chest: 36 (38, 40) inches

Sleeve length: 17½ (18½, 18½) inches

Materials

- Plymouth Encore worsted weight 75 percent acrylic/25 percent wool yarn (200 yds/100g per ball): 3 balls green #054, 1 ball soft white #146, 2 (2, 3) balls orange #1383, 2 balls medium charcoal #389, 1 ball yellow #1014
- Size 5 (3.75mm) 16- and 24-inch circular needles
- Size 7 (4.5mm) 24-inch circular needle or size needed to obtain gauge
- Stitch markers
- Stitch holders
- Tapestry needle

Gauge

20 sts and 26 rows = 4 inches/10cm in St st with larger needles

To save time, take time to check gauge.

Pattern Note

Outlines and small details may be worked in duplicate st after knitting is completed, while larger areas should be worked using intarsia method.

Front

Beg at bottom with smaller needles and orange, cast on 84 (88, 92) sts.

Work in k1, p1 rib for 2½ inches, inc 8 (10, 10) sts evenly across last WS row. (92, 98, 102 sts)

Change to larger needles and work in St st, following front chart. Pm at each end of Row 88 (92, 94) as indicated for sleeve placement.

Shape neck

On Row 121 (123, 127), work across first 37 (40, 40) sts, place center 18 (18, 22) neck sts on holder, join 2nd ball of yarn, work across last 37 (40, 40) sts.

Working both sides at once, dec 1 st at each neck edge [every other row] 7 times, then work even through Row 140 (144, 146). Do not bind off.

Back

Row 1 (RS): With green, k 30 (33, 33) sts, cast on 32 (32, 36) sts, then k remaining 30 (33, 33) sts. (92, 98, 102 sts)

Work back in St st until 140 (144, 146) rows have been completed, marking armholes as for front.

Ribbing

Next row (RS): Change to smaller needles, k one row with orange, dec

8 (10, 10) sts evenly across. (84, 88, 92 sts)

Work in k1, p1 rib for 2½ inches. Bind off in pat.

Neck band

With smaller 16-inch needle and orange, pick up and k 19 (21, 19) sts along left front neck edge, k across center 18 (18, 22) sts, pick up and k 19 (21, 19) sts along right front neck edge, k across 32 (32, 36) back neck sts. (88, 92, 96 sts)

Join and work in k1, p1 rib for 3 inches. Bind off in pat, fold band in half to inside and sew in place.

Sleeves

With larger needles and medium charcoal, RS facing, pick up and k 82 (82, 84) sts between markers on sweater front and back.

Beg with Row 1 (WS), follow sleeve chart, dec as indicated. Complete chart through Row 98 (104, 104). (44, 48, 50 sts)

Change to smaller needles, with orange, purl across next row, dec 4 sts evenly across. (40, 44, 46 sts)

Work in k1, p1 rib for 2½ inches, then bind off in pat.

Sew sleeve and body seams. ❖

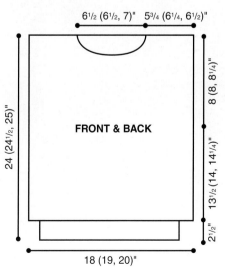

FRONT & BACK

6½ (6½, 7)" 5¾ (6¼, 6½)"

8 (8, 8¼)"

24 (24½, 25)"

13½ (14, 14¼)"

2½"

18 (19, 20)"

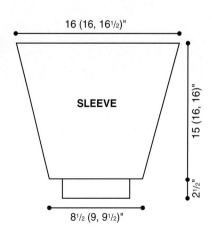

SLEEVE

16 (16, 16½)"

15 (16, 16)"

2½"

8½ (9, 9½)"

COLOR KEY
- ☐ Soft white
- ∧ Yellow
- ⅅ Orange
- ─ Green
- ◺ Medium charcoal
- ☒ Sleeve placement

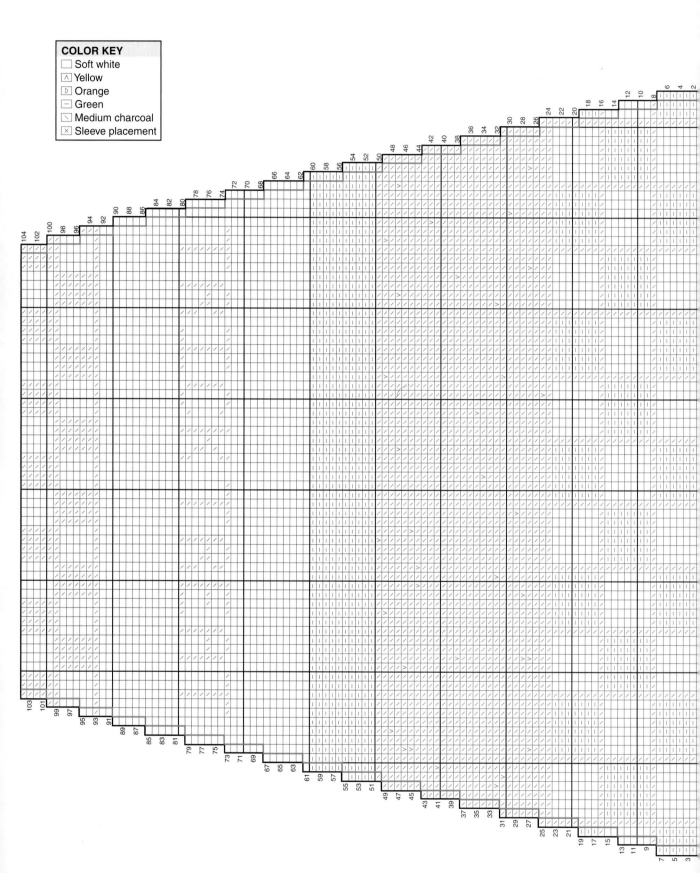

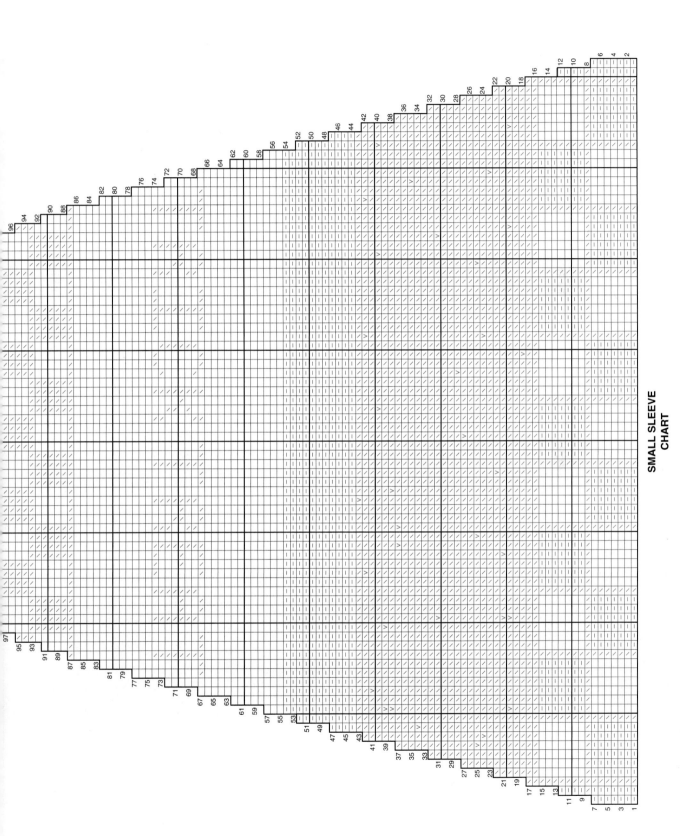

SMALL SLEEVE
CHART

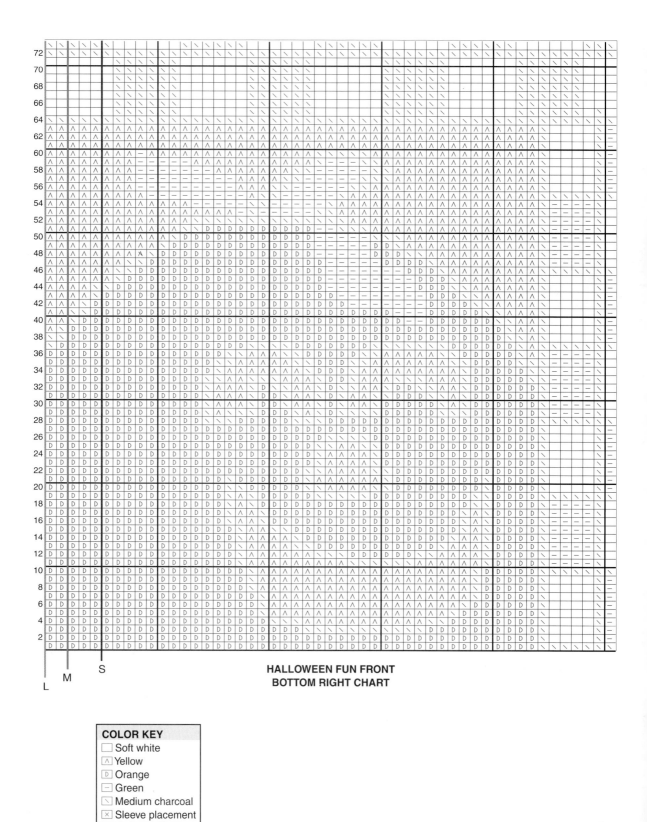

**HALLOWEEN FUN FRONT
BOTTOM RIGHT CHART**

COLOR KEY
- ☐ Soft white
- ⋀ Yellow
- D Orange
- ⚊ Green
- ⧵ Medium charcoal
- ⊠ Sleeve placement

**HALLOWEEN FUN FRONT
BOTTOM LEFT CHART**

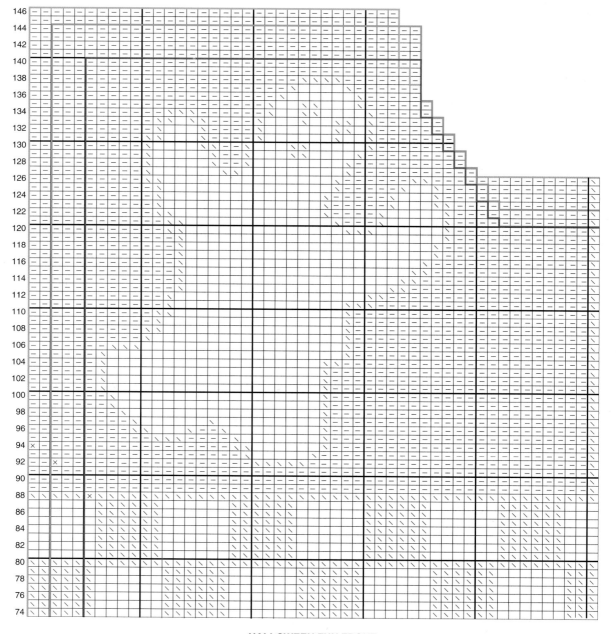

HALLOWEEN FUN FRONT
TOP RIGHT CHART

COLOR KEY
Soft white
⋀ Yellow
D Orange
− Green
⟍ Medium charcoal
✕ Sleeve placement

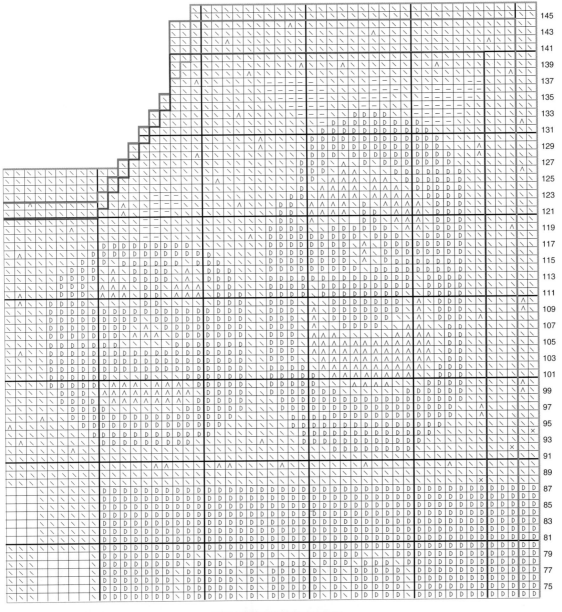

**HALLOWEEN FUN FRONT
TOP LEFT CHART**

Cuff-to-Cuff Kid

Design by Katharine Hunt

A buttoned shoulder and textured slip stitch make this colorful sweater
with a saw-toothed border a delight to knit for your child.

Skill Level
Intermediate***

Size
Child's 18–24 months (2, 4)
Instructions are given for smallest
size, with larger sizes in parentheses.
When only 1 number is given,
it applies to all sizes.

Finished Measurements
Chest: 26 (29, 32) inches
Length: 12 (13¾, 15¼) inches
(excluding edging)

Materials
- Plymouth Encore DK weight 75
  percent acrylic/25 percent wool
  yarn (150 yds/50g per ball): 2 (3,
  3) balls red #1386, 2 (3, 3) balls
  orange #1383, 1 ball each yellow
  #1382, purple #1384
- Size 3 (3.25mm) straight and
  16-inch circular needles
- Size 7 (4.5mm) needles or size
  needed to obtain gauge
- Tapestry needle

Gauge
24 sts and 42 rows = 4 inches/10cm
in pat with larger needles

To save time, take time to check
gauge.

Pattern Notes
Garment is knit sideways in 1 piece,
from left cuff to right cuff. Bottom
border is worked separately, and
sewn on after garment is completed.

Slip all sl sts purlwise wyib. Strand
will be on WS on Row 1 and on RS
on Row 2. When a RS row starts with
a sl st, take yarn to back, across RS
of first st before slipping it. Yarn is
then in place to knit 2nd st.

When inc and dec on sleeves, work
inc or dec 1 st in from edge. Be
sure to maintain pat so that all sl
sts and all knit sts are aligned above
each other.

Carry colors most frequently used,
(red and orange) up side of work,
looping them in on RS rows with
working color. To prevent bulk, cut
less frequently used colors, (yellow
and purple) and reattach as needed.

When sewing up, take care to sew
into fabric edge and not into yarn
carried up side of work.

Pattern Stitches
Slip Stitch Pat (multiple of 2 sts + 1)
Rows 1 and 2: K1, *sl 1 wyib, k1,
rep from * to end of row.
Row 3: Knit.
Row 4: Purl.
Rep Rows 1–4 in color sequence
as indicated.

Border
With smaller needles and red,
cast on 5 sts.
Row 1 (RS): K2, yo, k3.
Rows 2, 4 and 6: Knit.
Row 3: K2, yo, k4.
Row 5: K2, yo, k5.
Row 7: K2, yo, k6.
Row 8: Bind off 4 sts, k to end.
Rep to required length and bind off
on Row 8.

Cuff
Beg at left cuff with red and smaller
needles, cast on 43 (45, 51) sts and
k 7 rows, inc 1 st at each end of last
row. Purl 1 row (WS).

Change to orange and larger needles,
work Rows 1–4 of pat, inc 1 st on
each side on 3rd row.

Continue with yellow, orange, red,
purple, red stripes, inc on Row 3 of
every other stripe until there are 55
(57, 63) sts, then inc on Row 3 of
every stripe until there are 73 (77,

83) sts on needle. Work to end of
Row 2 of 19th (22nd, 27th) stripe
(not counting cuff). Break yarn.

Body
Row 3: On empty needle, with same
color, cast on 36 (43, 49) sts, k 73
(77, 83) sts from left needle, then cast
on 36 (43, 49) sts. (145, 163, 181 sts)
Turn. Purl to end. Change to next
color and continue in pat.

*Note: After 5th (5th, 6th) purple
stripe from beg, stripe sequence
changes to red/orange/yellow/
orange. Purple is not used again
until corresponding position on
other side of neckline.*

Beg shoulder opening
Complete 4 (4, 5) more stripes after
inc stripe, plus first 3 rows of next
stripe. Mark center st with a pin.

Next row: P69 (78, 87), bind off 4 sts
(3 sts before center st, plus center
st), p to end of row.

Join new balls for 2nd side, and
working both sides at once with
separate balls, continue in color
sequence for 5 (6, 6) more stripes.

Shape neck
On Row 3 of next stripe, k across
back to neck edge. Bind off 9 sts at
beg of 2nd side (front neck edge), k
to end. On next row, p to end of first
side, then bind off 2 sts at back neck
edge on 2nd side.

On following rows, maintaining color
sequence, bind off 1 st at back neck
edge [every row] 3 times, and 1 st
at front neck edge [every RS row]
4 (5, 6) times.

Work even for 7 (9, 11) more stripes
plus 2 rows of next stripe.

Reverse neck shapings by inc 1 st at
front neck edge [every RS row] 4 (5,
6) times, and 1 st at back neck edge
on last 3 rows.

Next row: Work first side, cast on

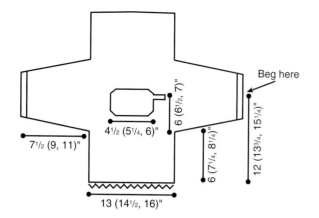

Diagram labels:
Beg here
6 (6½, 7)"
4½ (5¼, 6)"
7½ (9, 11)"
6 (7¼, 8¼)"
12 (13¾, 15¼)"
13 (14½, 16)"

15 sts, with same ball, work to end. (145, 163, 181 sts)

Work same number and sequence of stripes up to edge of body as on other side.

Bind off body

At beg of next 2 rows, bind off 36 (43, 49) sts, work to end. (73, 77, 83 sts)

Continue in pat on 2nd sleeve,

following same stripe sequence as previous sleeve, and dec on Row 3 of every stripe until 55 (57, 63) sts remain, then Row 3 of every other stripe until 45 (47, 53) sts remain, ending stripe sequence on a 4th orange row.

Cuff

Change to red and smaller needles,

k 7 rows, dec 1 st at each end of first row. Bind off knitwise on WS.

Finishing

Neck band

With circular needle and red, RS facing, pick up and k 9 sts along left front neck edge, 28 (34, 40) sts across front edge from start to end of shaping, 15 sts along right neck edge, and 34 (40, 48) sts across back neck. (86, 98, 112 sts)

Do not join, but work back and forth in rows.

Next row (WS): K, dec 3 (4, 5) sts evenly across back and 2 (3, 4) sts on front. (81, 91, 103 sts)

K 5 rows, dec 4 (5, 6) sts evenly across front on last row. (77, 86, 97 sts)

Bind off knitwise on WS.

Buttonhole band

With red and smaller needles, pick up and k 21 (24, 24) sts along left front shoulder and neck-band edge. K 3 rows.

Row 4 (RS): Make 3 buttonholes, k3 (4, 4), bind off 2, [k5 (6, 6), bind off 2] twice, k to neck edge.

Row 5: K, casting on 2 sts over each bound off pair.

K 1 row, then bind off knitwise on WS.

Button band

Work as for buttonhole band, picking up sts along back neck band edge and left back shoulder, omitting buttonholes.

Lap buttonhole band over button band and sew in place.

Block by pinning out to size on a clean padded surface. Cover with a damp cloth and leave overnight to dry. Do not press.

Sew right sleeve and body seam.

Border

With red and smaller needles, work border pattern to fit bottom edge of tunic. Do not bind off.

Beg at left side edge, sew border to bottom edge of tunic to within a few inches of end. Check length, and add or shorten as required. Bind off border. Finish sewing border to edge.

Sew left sleeve and body seam, including ends of border. ❖

A Beach Holiday

Summer Swing Top

Design by Lois S. Young

You will be swinging to the tunes of summer in this cool top.
The diagonal hem and neckline will show off just a bit of your new summer tan.

Skill Level
Easy**

Size
Woman's small (medium, large)
Instructions are given for smallest size, with larger sizes in parentheses. If only 1 number is given, it applies to all sizes.

Finished Measurements
Chest: 33 (37, 41) inches

Length: 16½ (18, 19½) inches (center back neck to center back waist)

Materials
- Plymouth Wildflower DK weight 51 percent mercerized cotton/49 percent acrylic yarn (137 yds/50g per ball): 4 (5, 6) balls peach #13 (MC), 1 ball each sage #20 (A), off-white #40 (B)
- Size 3 (3.25mm) straight and 16-inch circular needles or size needed to obtain gauge
- Stitch markers
- Tapestry needle

Gauge
24 sts and 32 rows = 4 inches/10cm in St st

To save time, take time to check gauge.

Pattern Note
Front and back are mirror images of each other.

Front
With straight needles and MC, cast on 60 (63, 66) sts. Work 8 (10, 12) rows St st, ending with a WS row, for underarm.

Shape armhole & beg slanted edge of bottom
Beg with RS row and continuing to work in St st throughout, inc 1 st at beg of row [every other row] 4 times to shape armhole, and *at the same time,* dec 1 st at end of row [every 8th row] 0 (1, 2) times, then [every 6th row] 3 (2, 1) times to slant bottom. Only 2 (1, 1) of bottom (left edge) decs will have been worked when armhole incs are completed. (62, 66, 69 sts)

Beg shoulder strap
At end of next WS row, cast on 44 (47, 50) sts for shoulder strap. (106, 113, 119 sts)

Shape final armhole & underarm

Dec 1 st at beg of RS rows 4 times while continuing to dec at end of row. (35, 38, 41 sts)

Work 8 rows even. Bind off all sts.

Back

Cast on 35 (38, 41) sts. Work 8 (10, 12) rows even for underarm.

Shape armhole & beg slanted edge of bottom

Beg on next row, inc 1 st at beg (right edge) [every other row] 4 times to shape armhole, and *at the same time,* inc 1 st at end (left edge) [every 8th row] 0 (1, 2) times and [every 6th row] 3 (2, 1) times to slant bottom. Only 2 (1, 1) of bottom (left edge) incs will have been worked when armhole incs are completed. (41, 43, 46 sts)

Beg shoulder strap

At end of last WS row, cast on 44 (47, 50) sts for shoulder strap. (85, 90, 96 sts)

Work 10 (12, 14) rows for strap, working last 1 (2, 2) incs at bottom edge.

Shape neck

At beg of next RS row, bind off 14 (17, 20) sts. (72, 75, 78 sts)

On next RS row, dec 1 st at right edge and inc 1 at left edge, then rep [every 4th row] 18 (20, 22) times.

Beg 2nd shoulder strap

At end of next WS row, cast on 33 (36, 39) sts for shoulder strap. (105, 111, 117 sts)

Work 10 (12, 14) rows, continuing to inc at left edge [every 6th row] 3 (2, 1) times. Only first 1 (2, 2) incs will be made while shoulder strap is being worked. Bind off 44 (47, 50) sts at end of shoulder strap rows. (62, 66, 69 sts)

Shape armhole & underarm

Dec 1 st at right edge on RS rows 4 times while continuing with left edge incs. (60, 63, 66 sts)

Work 8 (10, 12) rows even. Bind off all sts. Sew shoulder seams.

Finishing

Armhole border

With 16-inch circular needle and A, RS facing, pick up and k 14 (16, 18) sts along underarm and curved edge

---

Work 10 (12, 14) rows for strap, working last 1 (2, 2) decs at bottom edge.

Shape neck

At beg of next RS row, bind off 33 (36, 39) sts. (72, 75, 78 sts)

On next RS row, inc 1 st at beg and dec 1 st at end, then rep [every 4th row] 18 (20, 22) times.

Beg 2nd shoulder strap

At end of next WS row, cast on 14 (17, 20) sts for shoulder strap. (86, 92, 98 sts)

Work 10 (12, 14) rows, continuing to dec at left edge [every 6th row] 3 (2, 1) times, then [every 8th row] 0 (1, 2) times. Only first 1 (2, 2) decs will be made while shoulder strap is being worked. Bind off 44 (47, 50) sts at end of shoulder strap. (41, 43, 46 sts)

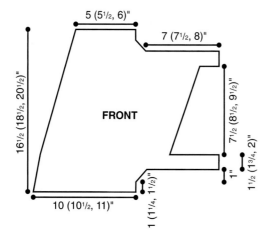

5 (5½, 6)"

7 (7½, 8)"

16½ (18½, 20½)"

FRONT

7½ (8½, 9½)"

1"

1½ (1¾, 2)"

10 (10½, 11)"

1 (1¼, 1½)"

of armhole, 43 (46, 49) sts along straight edge to shoulder, 43 (46, 49) sts down 2nd straight edge, and 14 (16, 18) sts along final curved edge and underarm. Work back and forth in k garter st, working 3 rows A, 4 rows B and 3 rows MC. On all RS rows, k6, k2tog, k to last 8 sts, ssk, k6. When last row of MC is completed, bind off knitwise on WS with MC. Work 2nd armhole border.

Bottom border

With regular needles and A, RS of back facing, pick up and k 99 (113, 127) sts. Knit back and forth in same color sequence as armhole. On final RS row of each color, dec 1 st on short side seam edge and inc 1 st on long side seam edge. When last row of MC is completed, bind off knitwise on WS with MC.

Work border on front to match back, reversing inc and dec sts at side seams on last RS row of each color. Sew side seams.

Neck border

Beg at back right shoulder (longer shoulder strap). With circular needle and A, RS facing, pick up and k 33 (36, 39) sts, pm for deep corner, 59 (66, 73) sts across back neck, pm for shallow corner, 13 (16, 19) sts to shoulder and 13 (16, 19) sts along strap to front neck, pm for shallow corner, 59 (66, 73) sts across neck front, pm for deep corner, 33 (36, 39) sts along remaining strap. K each row using same color sequence as for armholes.

Row 1 (WS): K to 2 sts before deep corner marker, k2tog, k to shallow corner marker, k2tog, k to 2 sts before shallow corner marker, k2tog, k to deep corner marker, k2tog, k to end of row.

Row 2: K to 2 sts before deep corner, k2tog, k3tog, k to 2 sts before shallow corner marker, k2tog, k to shallow corner marker, k2tog, k to 3 sts before deep corner marker, k3tog, k2tog, k to end of row.

Rows 3, 5, 7 and 9: Knit.

Row 4: K to 2 sts before deep corner marker, k2tog, k3tog, k to 2 sts before shallow corner marker, ssk, k2tog, k to 2 sts before shallow corner marker, ssk, k2tog, k to 3 sts before deep corner marker, k3tog,

k2tog, k to end of row.

Row 6: K to deep corner marker, k3tog, k past 2 shallow corner markers, k to 3 sts before deep corner marker, k3tog, k to end of row.

Row 8: K to 2 sts before deep corner marker, ssk, k1, k2tog, k to 3 sts before shallow corner marker, ssk, k1, k2tog, k to 2 sts before shallow corner marker, ssk, k1, k2tog, k to 3 sts before deep corner marker, ssk, k1, k2tog, k to end of row.

Row 10: K to deep corner marker, k3tog, k to 3 sts before shallow corner marker, ssk, k1, k2tog, k to 2 sts before shallow corner marker, ssk, k1, k2tog, k to 3 sts before deep corner marker, k3tog, k to end of row.

Bind off all sts, working corners as [bind off to 1 st before marker, sl 1, remove marker, replace sl st on LH needle, k2tog], continue with bind off. Sew seam of neck border. ❖

Blue Jeans Beach Vest

Design by Kennita Tully

This stylish vest is worked in one piece from side to side. The combination of yarns and the slip-stitch mesh pattern stitch make this vest very attractive.

Skill Level
Easy**

Size
Woman's small (medium, large)
Instructions are given for smallest size, with larger sizes in parentheses. When only 1 number is given, it applies to all sizes.

Finished Measurements
Chest: 36 (40, 44) inches
Length: 19 (20, 21) inches

Materials
- Plymouth Blu Jeans DK weight 100 percent indigo dyed cotton yarn (118 yds/50g per skein): 7 (7, 8) skeins light blue #2 (MC), 2 (2, 3) skeins natural #1 (CC)
- Size 5 (3.75mm) 24-inch circular needle
- Size 6 (4mm) needles or size needed to obtain gauge
- Stitch markers
- Tapestry needle
- 4 (¾-inch) buttons

Gauge
22 sts and 38 rows = 4 inches/10cm in pat with larger needles

To save time, take time to check gauge.

Pattern Notes
Vest is worked in 1 piece from side to side, beg at left center front.

Dec by k or p last 2 sts tog as indicated by pat. Inc by k in front and back of edge st, except on Row 3, pick up and k blue bar of sl st 1 st in from end, and on Row 5, work an extra yo.

Special Abbreviation
Rev St st (reverse St st): Purl on RS rows, knit on WS rows.

Right side of vest

Wrong side of vest

Pattern Stitch

Sl St Mesh (even number of sts)

Row 1 (RS): With MC, purl.

Row 2: With MC, knit.

Row 3: With CC, k3, *sl 1 wyib, k1, rep from *, end k1.

Row 4: With CC, k2, *sl 1 wyif, k1, rep from *, end k2.

Row 5: With MC, k2, *yo, k2 tog, rep from *, end k2.

Row 6: With MC, purl.

Rep Rows 1–6 for pat.

Vest

Cast on 72 (78, 84) sts.

Shape neck

Beg with Row 1 of pat, and marking end of Row 1 for neck edge, inc 1 st at neck edge [every row] 32 times. (104, 110, 116 sts)

Work even for 3 (4, 4½) inches after shaping is

104 (110, 116) sts for approximately 12 (14, 16) inches, placing markers for shoulder seams at 3 (4, 4½) inches and 9 (10, 11½) inches, ending with Row 1.

Shape 2nd armhole

Rep shaping for right armhole. When sts have been cast on for right front, work approximately 3 (4, 4½) inches, ending with Row 3.

Shape neck

Dec for V-neck by dec 1 st at neck edge [every row] 32 times, ending with Row 6. (72, 78, 84 sts)

Work 1 more RS row, then bind off all sts.

Finishing

Wash and press to measurements. Seam shoulders between markers.

With smaller needles and MC, RS facing, pick up and k 180 (200, 220) sts and work 4 rows of rev St st. Bind off all sts.

Armband

With smaller needles and MC, RS facing, pick up and k 84 (92, 104) sts around armhole, work 4 rows in rev st st. Bind off all sts. Rep for other armhole.

Front band

Beg at bottom right corner with smaller needles and MC, RS facing, pick up and k 18 (24, 30) sts along right front, [skip 3 sts, cast on 3 sts, pick up and k 13 sts] 3 times, skip 3 sts, cast on 3 sts, pick up and k 3 sts to beg of neck shaping, 29 sts along neck edge, 27 (27, 32) across back neck, 29 along left neck edge and 72 (78, 84) sts along left front edge. (229, 241, 258 sts)

Work 4 rows rev St st and bind off all sts. Sew on buttons to correspond to buttonholes. ❖

completed, ending with Row 1 or 5.

Shape armhole

At beg of next WS row (Row 2 or 6), bind off 26 (30, 36) sts.

Continuing in pat, dec 1 st at armhole edge [every other row] 5 (6, 6) times, then [every row] twice. (71, 72, 72 sts)

Work even for 22 (28, 28) rows then reverse shaping for other side of armhole by inc 1 st at armhole edge [every row] twice, then [every other row] 5 (6, 6) times.

At end of next RS row (Row 5), cast on 26 (30, 36) sts and work even on

VEST

19 (20, 21)"

3¼"

6 (7, 8)"

6 (6, 7)"

3 (4, 4½)"

13"

3 (4, 4½)"

36 (40, 44)"

5¾"   13¼ (14¼, 15¼)"

Summer Tea Top

Design by Diane Zangl

For fun in the sun, here is a quick and easy summer top
that's knit all in one piece, with only two seams to sew.

Skill Level

Advanced****

Size

Woman's extra-small (small, medium, large) Instructions are given for smallest size, with larger sizes in parentheses. When only 1 number is given, it applies to all sizes.

Finished Measurements

Chest: 34 (38, 42, 46) inches

Armhole depth: 8 (8½, 9, 10) inches

Side to underarm: 13 (13, 14, 14½) inches

Sleeve length: 3 (3, 3½, 3½) inches

Materials

- Plymouth Wildflower DK weight 51 percent mercerized cotton/49 percent acrylic yarn (137 yds/50g per ball): 4 (4, 5, 6) balls white #41, 2 (2, 3, 3) balls parakeet #55, 1 (2, 2, 2) balls yellow #48
- Size 4 (3.5mm) 16- and 24-inch circular needles
- Size 6 (4mm) needles or size needed to obtain gauge
- Stitch holders
- Stitch markers
- Tapestry needle

Gauge

21 sts and 28 rows = 4 inches/10cm in St st with larger needles

To save time, take time to check gauge.

Special Abbreviations

K1-b: K1 in back loop.

P1-b: P1 in back loop.

Wrap: Bring yarn to front of work, sl 1 purlwise, take yarn to back of work, replace sl st to LH needle. On next row, work wrap with main st.

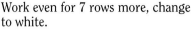

Pattern Stitch

1/1 Twisted Rib (odd number of sts)

Row 1 (RS): K1-b, *p1, k1-b, rep from * across.

Row 2: P1-b, *k1, p1-b, rep from * across.

Rep Rows 1 and 2 for pat.

Pattern Notes

Use separate balls of yarn or bobbins for each color section on front.

To avoid holes when changing colors, always bring new color up over old.

Left Sleeve

With smaller needles and yellow, cast on 71 (75, 79, 87) sts.

Work even in 1/1 Twisted Rib for 1½ inch, inc 13 (15, 15, 17) sts evenly on last WS row. (84, 90, 94, 104 sts)

Change to blue and larger needles. Work even in St st for 1½ (1½, 2, 2) inches, ending with a WS row.

Shape sleeve cap

Rows 1 and 2: Work to last 10 sts, wrap next st, turn.

Rows 3–6: Work to 10 sts before previous wrap, wrap next st, turn.

Rows 7–8: Work to 5 sts before previous wrap, wrap next st, turn.

Rows 9–10: Work across row, working each wrap tog with main st.

Body

Cast on 60 (60, 66, 68) sts at end of next 2 rows. (204, 210, 226, 240 sts)

Work even until body measures 6 (6½, 7, 7¾) inches above cast-on body sts, ending with a WS row.

Change to yellow.

Back neck

Next row: K97 (100, 108, 115), sl remaining sts to holder.

Work even for 7 rows more, change to white.

Work even in St st until back neck measures 5 (6, 7, 7½) inches above yellow stripe, ending with a WS row. Sl back sts to holder.

Front neck

Sl sts from first holder to needle. With RS facing, join blue at back neck.

Bind off 22 (23, 24, 25) sts, cut blue, join yellow, ssk, k to end of row.

Dec 1 st at neck edge [every other row] 3 times more. Purl 1 row.

Change to white.

Next row (RS): K25 white, k6 yellow, attach 2nd ball of white, k to end of row.

Work even in established colors until front neck measures 2¾ (3¾, 4¾, 5¼) inches above yellow horizontal stripe, ending with a WS row.

[Inc 1 st at neck edge every other row] 4 times. Purl 1 row.

Join front and back

Sl back sts from holder to LH needle. K97 (100, 108, 115), cast on 22 (23, 24, 25) sts for right side of neck, work in established color pat to end of row. (204, 210, 226, 240 sts)

Work even until right side of body measures 6 (6½, 7, 7¾) inches above cast-on neck sts, ending with a WS row.

Right Sleeve

Bind off 60 (60, 66, 68) sts at beg of next 2 rows. (84, 90, 94, 104 sts)

Shape sleeve cap

Row 1 (RS): K 48 (54, 58, 68) sts, wrap next st, turn.

Row 2: P13, (19, 23, 33), wrap next st, turn.

Rows 3–4: Work to 4 sts beyond last wrap, wrap next st, turn.

Rows 5–8: Work to 9 sts beyond last wrap, wrap next st, turn.

Row 9–10: Work to end of row, working each wrap tog with main st.

Work even on all sts for 1½ (1½, 2, 2) inches.

Change to smaller needles and yellow. Work even in 1/1 Twisted Rib for 1½ inches, dec 13 (15, 15, 17) sts evenly on first row. (71, 75, 79, 87 sts)

Bind off in pat.

Finishing

Neck band

With smaller 16-inch circular needle and yellow, pick up and k around neckline at a ratio of 2 sts for every 3 rows, and 4 sts for every 5 cast-on or bound-off sts. You must have an even number of sts. Pm between first and last st.

Rnds 1–7: *K1-b, p1, rep from * around.

Bind off in pat.

Sew sleeve and side seams.

Bottom band

With smaller 24-inch circular needle and white, pick up and k 2 sts for every 3 rows around bottom edge.

Work band as for neck band for 1½ inches. Bind off in pat. ❖

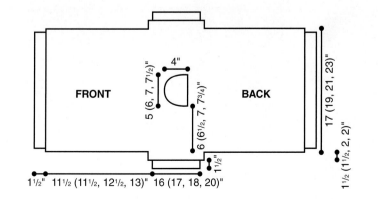

FRONT   BACK

5 (6, 7, 7½)"   4"   6 (6½, 7, 7¾)"   17 (19, 21, 23)"   1½ (1½, 2, 2)"   1½"

1½"   11½ (11½, 12½, 13)"   16 (17, 18, 20)"

Amigo Top

Design by Diane Zangl

Friends will admire your fashion flair when you wear this stylish, sleeveless sweater. Knit from back to front in one piece, the V-shaped insert and bright yarns make this sweater one-of-a-kind.

Skill Level

Intermediate***

Size

Woman's small (medium, large, extra-large) Instructions are given for smallest size, with larger sizes in parentheses. When only 1 number is given, it applies to all sizes.

Finished Measurements

Chest: 38 (42, 46, 50) inches

Side to underarm: 10½ (10½, 11½, 11½) inches

Armhole depth: 8 (9, 9½, 9½) inches

Materials

- Plymouth Wildflower Fancy DK weight 53 percent acrylic/43 percent cotton/4 percent nylon (116 yds/50g per ball): 5 (5, 6, 7) balls white confetti #841 (MC)
- Plymouth Wildflower DK weight 51 percent mercerized cotton/49 percent acrylic yarn (137 yds/50g per ball): 2 (2, 3, 3) balls bright pink #59 (CC)
- Size 4 (3.5mm) 16- and 24-inch circular needles
- Size 6 (4mm) needles or size needed to obtain gauge
- Stitch markers
- Tapestry needle

Gauge

21 sts and 29 rows = 4 inches/10cm in St st with larger needles

Note: *Row gauge must be accurate in this pat.*

To save time, take time to check gauge.

Pattern Note

To avoid holes when changing colors, always bring new color up over old.

Left Back

Beg at center back with MC and larger needles, cast on 89 (95, 103, 103) sts, using any provisional method.

Row 1 (WS): P to last 4 sts, k4.

Row 2: Sl 1 purlwise wyif, p3, k to end of row.

Rep these 2 rows until back measures 9½ (10½, 11½, 12½) inches, ending with a WS row.

Shape armhole

Bind off 42 (47, 50, 50) sts at beg of next row. Mark end of this row.

Left Front

P47 (48, 53, 53) MC, with CC, cast on 42 (47, 50, 50) sts.

Beg panel shaping

Row 1 (RS): Sl 1, p3, k to last st of CC, p1, k1; with MC, k to end of row.

Row 2: With MC, p to 1 st before CC; with CC, p1, k1, p to last 4 sts, k4.

Continue in this manner, adding 1 more st in CC every row until all MC sts have been worked.

Work even in CC only until left front measures same as left back when measured above marker. Count number of rows worked in CC only and record.

Right Front

Work even in CC for number of recorded rows.

Beg panel shaping

Row 1 (RS): With CC, sl 1, p3, k to last 2 sts of CC, p1; with MC, p to end of row.

Row 2: With MC, p to include first st of CC; with CC, k1, p to last 4 sts, k4.

Rep these 2 rows until there are 47 (48, 53, 53) sts in MC and 42 (47, 50, 50) sts in CC.

Shape armhole

Next row (WS): Bind off 42 (47, 50, 50) CC sts, k to end of row. Mark this row, cut CC.

Right Back

Next row: With MC, purl, cast on 42

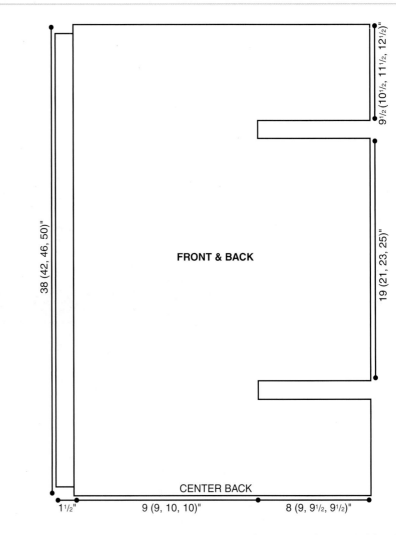

(47, 50, 50) sts. (89, 95, 103, 103 sts)

Keeping 4 sts at top edge in rolled sts as before, work even in St st until right back measures same as left back when measured above marked row. Do not bind off. Cut yarn leaving a long end for sewing.

Weave back seam using Kitchener st.

Finishing

Bottom band

Beg at center back with MC and smaller 24-inch circular needle, pick up and k 2 sts for every 3 rows around bottom of sweater. You must have an even number of sts. Pm between first and last st.

Next rnd: *K1-b, p1, rep from * around.

Work even in rib pat until band measures 1½ inches.

Bind off in pat.

Sew shoulder seams for 4½ (5¼, 5¾, 6½) inches. With WS of pieces tog, sew seam from RS in 4th st from edge, allowing rolled sts to curl naturally to RS of garment.

Armband

Beg at underarm with MC and smaller 16-inch circular needle, pick up and k 4 sts for every 5 sts around armhole, and going through both layers of shoulder roll. You must have an even number of sts. Pm between first and last st.

Work armband as for bottom until band measures 1 inch. Bind off in pat. ❖

Chevron Lace Top

Design by E. J. Slayton

You'll feel as delicate as a wildflower in this lacy cotton blouse.
The airy design will help you stay cool on those hot summer days.

Skill Level
Intermediate***

Size
Woman's small (medium, large, extra-large) Instructions are given for smallest size, with larger sizes in parentheses. When only 1 number is given, it applies to all sizes.

Finished Measurements
Chest: 35 (38½, 42, 45½) inches
Length: 19 (19, 21, 21) inches

Materials
• Plymouth Wildflower DK weight 51 percent mercerized cotton/49 percent acrylic yarn (137 yds/50g per ball): 6 (7, 7, 8) balls natural #40
• Size 3 (3.25mm) needles or size needed to obtain gauge
• Stitch markers
• Stitch holders
• Tapestry needle

Gauge
23 sts and 30 rows = 4 inches/10cm in pat
To save time, take time to check gauge.

Pattern Notes
Instructions and yarn amounts are given for a slightly cropped length. For longer top, continue working to desired length, and add 1 ball to yarn amounts given.

When shaping or working new sts into pat, maintain at least a 2-st St st selvage at each edge.

To make it easier to keep track of shaping, work both sleeves at once with separate balls of yarn.

Special Abbreviation
CDD (central double decrease): Sl next 2 sts as if to k2tog, k1, p2sso.

M1 (make 1): Inc by making a backward loop over right needle.

Pattern Stitch
Chevron Lace (multiple of 15 sts)
Row 1 and all WS rows: Purl.
Row 2: *K3, k2tog, k2, yo, k1, yo, k2, ssk, k3, rep from * across.
Row 4: *K2, k2tog, k2, yo, k3, yo, k2, ssk, k2, rep from * across.
Row 6: *K1, k2tog, k2, yo, k5, yo, k2, ssk, k1, rep from * across.
Row 8: *K2tog, k2, yo, k7, yo, k2, ssk, rep from * across.
Rep Rows 1–8 for pat.

Back
Beg at top, cast on 81 (87, 95, 101) sts. Knit 4 rows.

Beg pat: Purl across.

Row 2: K3 (6, 2, 5), pm, beg as indicated on chart, work Row 2 of pat across 75 (75, 91, 91) sts, pm, end k3 (6, 2, 5).

Continue to work in pat until piece measures 6 (6, 6½, 7) inches from beg, ending with a WS row.

Shape armhole
Continue to work in pat, inc 1 st at each edge [every RS row] 6 times. (93, 99, 107, 113 sts)

At beg of next 2 rows, cast on 5 (6, 7, 9) sts. (103, 111, 121, 131 sts)

Note: *Due to size of rep, there will be 7 (3, 1, 6) sts in St st at each edge of body.*

Work in pat until body measures 11 (11, 12, 12) inches or approximately 1 inch less than desired length from underarm, ending with Row 8.

Border
Work Rows 1–8 of lace pat, knitting all WS rows, and working M1 in place of each yo. Knit 1 row, then bind off in purl on RS.

Front
With RS facing, beg at right shoulder and working in cast on edge, pick up and k 20 (23, 25, 28) sts, mark center 41 (41, 45, 45) sts for neck; join 2nd ball of yarn, pick up and k 20 (23, 25, 28) sts for left shoulder. Working both sides at once, k 4 rows.

Beg pat as for back, keeping neck edge sts in St st. Work [pat Rows 1–8] twice, rep Row 1.

Shape neck
Maintaining pat and beg on next row, inc 1 st at each neck edge [every RS row] 5 times. On next RS row, work across right shoulder, cast on 31 (31, 35, 35) sts for front neck, cut 2nd ball of yarn, and complete row.

Complete front as for back.

14 (15, 16½, 17½)"

7 (7, 7¾, 7¾)"

FRONT & BACK

7 (7, 8, 8)"

19 (19, 21, 21)"

12 (12, 13, 13)"

17½ (19¼, 21, 22¾)"

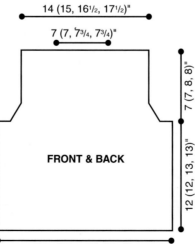

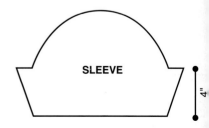

SLEEVE

4"

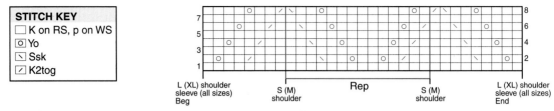

STITCH KEY

- ☐ K on RS, p on WS
- ☐ Yo
- ☐ Ssk
- ☐ K2tog

L (XL) shoulder
sleeve (all sizes)
Beg

S (M) shoulder

Rep

S (M) shoulder

L (XL) shoulder
sleeve (all sizes)
End

CHEVRON LACE CHART

Sleeves

Cast on 29 (29, 29, 31) sts. Mark center st.

Beg with a purl row, work in St st, casting on at end of each row [3 (3, 4, 4) sts] 6 times, then inc 1 st each side [every RS row] 14 times. (75, 75 81, 83 sts)

At the same time, beg on Row 4, work pat across center 31 sts, working new sts in St st until they can be worked into pat.

Shape underarm

At beg of row, cast on [5 (6, 7, 9) sts] twice. (85, 87, 95, 101 sts)

Maintaining pat, work until sleeve measures 1 inch from underarm, ending with a WS row.

Dec 1 st on each side every 6th row until sleeve measures 3 inches from underarm, ending with Row 8. Work border as for back. Bind off all sts in purl on RS.

Finishing

Neck band

With circular needle and RS facing, beg at right shoulder, pick up and k 41 (41, 45, 45) sts across cast on edge of back neck, pm, 2 sts for every 3 rows along left neck edge, 31 (31, 35 35) sts across cast on edge of front neck, marking first, center and last front neck sts with a safety pin, and 2 sts for every 3 rows along right neck edge, pm. Join and work in rnds.

Rnds 1 and 3: Purl.

Rnd 2: Knit, working 3 CDD's evenly across back neck, and at each marker across front neck.

Rnd 4: Knit, working CDD's across front neck only.

Rnd 5: Purl.

Bind off all sts in purl.

Set sleeves into armholes, then sew sleeve and body underarm seams.

Block lightly. ❖

Sand & Waves

Design by Edie Eckman

Wrap yourself in sunshine with this cheerful summer cardigan. This breezy sweater is stitched sideways, from the left sleeve cuff to the right.

Skill Level

Intermediate***

Size

Woman's small (medium, large) Instructions are given for smallest size, with larger sizes in parentheses. When only 1 number is given, it applies to all sizes.

Finished Measurements

Chest: 36 (42, 50) inches

Length: 22½ (23, 24) inches

Materials

- Plymouth Fantasy Naturale worsted weight 100 percent mercerized cotton yarn (140 yds/100g per skein): 11 (12, 14) skeins daffodil #1404
- Size 7 (4.5mm) 32-inch circular needle or size needed to obtain gauge
- Cable needle
- Waste yarn (for st holders)
- Tapestry needle
- Size F/5 (3.75mm) crochet hook
- 5 (¾-inch) buttons

Gauge

18 sts and 30 rows = 4 inches/10cm in St st after machine washing and drying (see Pattern Note)

To save time, take time to check gauge.

Pattern Note

Yarn shrinks after washing—be sure to wash a generous swatch as you intend to wash finished garment. The instructions have been written to accommodate the shrinkage factor. Because of this, instructions are given in row counts, rather than in inches. When counting rows, count long-tail cast-on row as 1 row.

Pattern Stitch

Seed St (odd number of sts)

All rows: *P1, k1, rep from * across.

Left Sleeve

Cast on 35 (37, 39) sts. Work 3 rows seed st. Beg on next row, inc 1 st each side [every 6th row] 12 (16, 20)

times then [every 8th row] 9 (6, 3) times, ending with a WS row. (77, 81 85 sts)

Work even until Row 147 is complete, ending with a WS row.

Body

With RS facing, continuing in

seed st, cast on 62 (64, 66) sts at beg of next 2 rows. (201, 209, 217 sts)

Working on back and front at same time, work 1 row seed st (RS) then beg Row 1 of cable pat from cable chart on first and last 15 sts of each row until Row 50 (60, 72) is completed.

Divide for neck

Continuing in established pats, work across 99 (103, 107) sts, place on holder. Bind off next 5 sts, work remaining 97 (101, 105) sts.

Left Front

Continuing in established pats, bind off at neck edge [2 sts] twice and [1 st] 4 times. Work even on 89 (93, 97) sts until 2 (3, 3) reps of cable pattern are completed, then work Rows 1–3 of cable pat again. Continue in seed st on all sts until 74 (86, 100) rows are completed from body cast on. Bind off all sts.

Right Front

Cast on 89 (93, 97) sts. Work in seed st, placing buttonholes on Row 4 and *at the same time,* beg Row 1 of cable pat on Row 17 (3, 17).

Buttonhole row: Mark 4th st from beg and 16th st from end, and 3 additional sts evenly spaced between these 2. [Work in pat to marker, yo, k2tog (or p2tog to maintain pat)] 4 times, work to end.

Work even in established pats through Row 11 (13, 15). Cast on 1 st at beg of next 4 RS rows and 2 sts at beg of following 2 RS rows for neck shaping. Place 97 (101, 105) sts on holder.

Back

Sl 99 (103, 107) sts from first holder onto needle. Continuing in established pats, bind off 2 sts at neck edge once, then work even on 97 (101, 105) sts for 42 rows. Cast on 2 sts at neck edge once, ending with a WS row.

Join front and back

On next row, with RS facing, work across back sts on needle, cast on 5 sts, work across 97 (101, 105) front sts. (201, 209, 217 sts)

Work even on all sts in established pats until 5 (6, 7) reps of cable pat are completed on back and 2 (3, 3) reps of cable pat on front, then rep Rows 1–3 of cable. If needed, change to seed st over first and last 15 sts of row after pat reps are completed, and work even until there are 144 (162, 188) rows on back, ending with a WS row. Bind off 62 (64, 66) sts at beg of next 2 rows. (77, 81, 85 sts)

Right Sleeve

Continuing in seed st, work even for 2 rows, then dec 1 st each side [every 8th row] 9 (6, 3) times, then [every 6th row] 12 (16, 20) times. Work

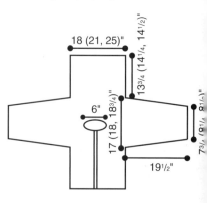

18 (21, 25)"

13¾ (14¼, 14½)"

6"

17 (18, 18¾)"

7¾ (8¼, 8½)"

19½"

even 3 rows. Bind off remaining 35 (37, 39) sts.

Finishing

Fold sweater and sew underarm and side seams. To improve stability, with WS facing, using purl bumps as a guide, with crochet hook sl st a shoulder "seam" from each neck edge across shoulder to beg of sleeve. Sl st around neck.

Sew buttons opposite buttonholes. Wash and dry sweater before wearing. ❖

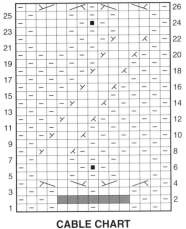

CABLE CHART

STITCH KEY

☐	K on RS, p on WS
–	P on RS, k on WS
■	Make bobble: [k1, p1, k1, p1, k1] into st, turn; p5, turn; k5, turn; p5, turn; pass 2nd, 3rd, 4th and 5th sts over first st, k1 tbl.
	C5R: Sl next 2 sts to cn, hold in back, k3, p2 from cn.
	C5L: Sl next 3 sts to cn, hold in front, p2, k3 from cn.
	C4R: Sl next st to cn, hold in back, k3, p1 from cn.
	7-St Cross: Sl next 4 sts to cn, hold in back, k3, return last st from cn to LH needle, p1, k3 from cn.

Beachcomber Pullover

Design by Lois S. Young

This unforgettable pullover is perfect for an evening stroll.
Work it from cuff to cuff, then pick up stitches and knit the body.

Skill Level
Intermediate***

Size
Man's small (medium, large, extra-large) Instructions are given for smallest size, with larger sizes in parentheses. If only 1 number is given, it applies to all sizes.

Finished Measurements
Chest: 40 (44, 48, 52) inches
Length: 25 (26, 27½, 29) inches

Materials
- Plymouth Fantasy Naturale worsted weight 100 percent mercerized cotton yarn (140 yds/100g per skein): 10 (11, 12, 13) skeins olive #5606
- Size 4 (3.5mm) needles
- Size 5 (3.75mm) 29-inch circular needle or size needed to obtain gauge
- Stitch markers
- Tapestry needle

Gauge
18 sts (2 pat reps) and 28 rows = 4 inches/10cm in pat with larger needles

To save time, take time to check gauge.

Pattern Notes
Work first and last 2 sts of all rows of body and yoke in garter st.

Keep sts in established pat as they are inc or dec at sides of sleeves and yoke. Shaping is worked inside the 2-st selvage on each side.

Special Abbreviations
RT (right twist): K1 in 2nd st on LH needle, leave st on needle, k1 in first st on LH needle, sl both sts off needle.

LT (left twist): With RH needle in back of work, k1 tbl of 2nd st on LH needle, leave st on needle, k1 in first st on LH needle, sl both sts off needle.

First Sleeve
With smaller 16-inch needle, cast on 36 (38, 42, 46) sts for cuff. Knit 16 rows, inc 8 (8, 10, 10) sts evenly on last row. (44, 46, 52, 56 sts)

Change to larger needle. Beg and ending as indicated, beg pat from chart. Working 2 sts in from edge, inc 1 st on each side [every 4th row] 12 (14, 16, 18) times, then [every 6th row] 8 times, working new sts into pat. (84, 90, 100, 108 sts)

Maintaining pat throughout, work even until sleeve measures 18 (19, 20, 21) inches from beg, ending with a WS row, pm in last row of sleeve. Make a note of number of rows between last inc row and end of sleeve.

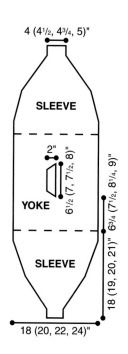

Yoke
Continue working for 6¾ (7½, 8¼, 9) inches for shoulder, ending with a WS row and again making a note of number of rows in this section of sweater.

Divide for front & back yoke
For back yoke, work back and forth on 42 (45, 50, 54) sts for 42 (46, 50, 54) rows, ending with WS row. Break yarn.

For front yoke, sl sts around on needle so that yarn can be attached at neck edge (RS row). Bind off 9 sts. (33, 36, 41, 45 sts)

Working back and forth, dec 1 st at neck edge [every RS row] 4 times. (29, 32, 37, 41 sts)

Work 27 (31, 35, 39) rows, ending with WS row. Inc 1 st at neck edge [every RS row] 4 times. (33, 36, 41, 45 sts)

Cast on 9 sts at beg of next WS row. (42, 45, 50, 54 sts)

Rejoin front and back yokes
Work back and forth across 84 (90, 100, 108) yoke sts until number of rows in 2nd shoulder matches first shoulder, ending with a WS row, pm to mark beg of sleeve.

Second Sleeve
Work back and forth until number of rows in top of sleeve matches first sleeve, ending with a WS row.

Working in same position as incs on first sleeve, dec 1 st each side on next RS row, then [every 6th row] 8 times, and [every 4th row] 11 (13, 15, 17) times. (44, 46, 52, 56 sts)

Work 4 rows even, ending with a WS row. Knit 1 row, dec 8 (8, 10, 10) sts evenly spaced. (36, 38, 42, 46 sts)

Change to smaller 16-inch needle. Knit 16 rows. Bind off knitwise on RS.

Sew sleeve seams.

End rnds for body

S (L)   M (XL)

Beg rnds for body

S (L)   M (XL)

XL   L   M S   ├── Rep ──┤   M   L   XL
End   S   Beg
sleeve   **BEACHCOMBER CHART**   sleeve

STITCH KEY
☐ K on RS, p on WS
⊟ P on RS, k on WS
⧄ LT
⧄ RT

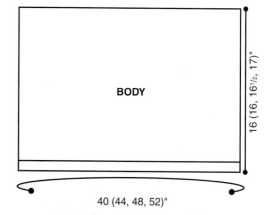

BODY

16 (16, 16½, 17)"

40 (44, 48, 52)"

Body

With larger needle and RS facing, pick up and k 180 (198, 216, 234) sts evenly spaced around yoke opening, pm for beg of rnd. Work pat in rnds until body measures 15 (15, 15½, 16) inches from underarms. [Purl 1 rnd, knit 1 rnd] 7 times. Purl 1 rnd. Bind off knitwise.

Neck Border

Using smaller 16-inch needle, beg at left shoulder with RS facing, pick up and k 16 sts along side neck, 16 (18, 20, 22) sts across front, 16 sts along side neck and 31 (33, 35, 37) sts across back. (79, 83, 87, 91 sts)

Work [purl 1 rnd, knit 1 rnd] 4 times. Purl 1 rnd. Bind off knitwise. ❖

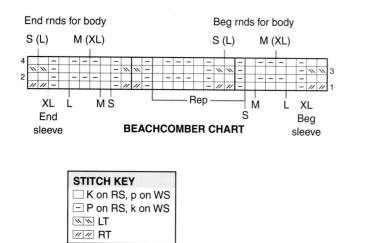

Rustic Cables

Design by Barbara Venishnick

This is the perfect sweater for an evening barbecue at the beach. It features an interesting pretzel-braid cable design, and is knit in a sideways pattern.

Skill Level
Intermediate***

Size
Small (medium, large) Instructions are given for smallest size, with larger sizes in parentheses. When only 1 number is given, it applies to all sizes.

Finished Measurements
Chest: 21½ (24½, 27½) inches
Length: 24 (24¾, 25¼) inches

Materials
- Plymouth Fantasy Naturale worsted weight 100 percent mercerized cotton yarn (140 yds/100g per skein): 9 (10, 11) skeins denim tweed #8003
- Size 8 (5mm) straight and 40-inch circular needles or size needed to obtain gauge
- Cable needle
- Tapestry needle

Gauge
16 sts and 22 rows = 4 inches/10cm in rib st
To save time, take time to check gauge.

Pattern Notes
Sweater is worked sideways from cuff to cuff. Sts are cast on then bound off for the side seams. The work is divided in half for the neck opening and both halves are worked at the same time, then joined for other side and sleeve.

Always maintain 1 selvage st on each side of work and at each side of neck opening. Selvage sts are included in st counts given.

Special Abbreviations
C4B: Sl 2 sts to cn, hold in back, k2, k2 from cn.

Row 1 (WS): Purl.

Row 2: *K2, p1, rep from * across.

Rep Rows 1 and 2 for rib pat.

Pretzel Braid (panel of 40 sts)

Row 1 (WS): [K4, p4] twice, k8, [p4, k4] twice.

Row 2: [P4, C4B] twice, p8, [C4B, p4] twice.

Row 3: Rep Row 1.

Row 4: P3, C3BP, C4FP, C4BP, C4FP, p4, C4BP, C4FP, C4BP, C3FP, p3.

Row 5: K3, p2, k3, p4, k4, [p2, k4] twice, p4, k3, p2, k3.

Row 6: P2, C3BP, p3, C4F, [p4, k2] twice, p4, C4F, p3, C3FP, p2.

Row 7: K2, p2, k4, p4,[k4, p2] twice, k4, p4, k4, p2, k2.

Row 8: P2, k2, p2, C4BP, C4FP, C4BP, p4, C4FP, C4BP, C4FP, p2, k2, p2.

Row 9: [K2, p2] twice, k4, p4, k8, p4, k4, [p2, k2] twice.

Row 10: [P2, k2] twice, p4, C4B, p8, C4B, p4, [k2, p2] twice.

Row 11: Rep Row 9.

Row 12: P2, k2, p2, C4FP, C4BP, C4FP, p4, C4BP, C4FP, C4BP, p2, k2, p2.

Row 13: Rep Row 7.

Row 14: P2, C3FP, p3, C4F, [p4, k2] twice, p4, C4F, p3, C3BP, p2.

Row 15: K3, p2, k3, p4, [k4, p2] twice, k4, p4, k3, p2, k3.

Row 16: P3, C3FP, C4BP, C4FP, C4BP, p4, C4FP, C4BP, C4FP, C3BP, p3.

C4F: Sl 2 sts to cn, hold in front, k2, k2 from cn.

C4BP: Sl 2 sts to cn, hold in back, k2, p2 from cn.

C4FP: Sl 2 sts to cn, hold in front, p2, k2 from cn.

C3BP: Sl 1 st to cn, hold in back, k2, p1 from cn.

C3FP: Sl 2 sts to cn, hold in front, p1, k2 from cn.

M1 (make 1): Inc by k1 in back of running thread between sts.

Sel st (selvage st): K1tbl at beg of every row, sl 1 st wyif at end of every row.

Special Technique

Cable cast on: *Insert RH needle between first and 2nd st on LH needle and draw up a loop, place this loop on LH needle, creating a new st, rep from * until desired number of sts has been cast on.

Pattern Stitches

Rib Pat (multiple of 3 sts; worked as a mirror image on each side of cable panel)

Before cable

Row 1 (WS): Purl.

Row 2: *P1, k2, rep from * across.

Rep Rows 1 and 2 for rib pat.

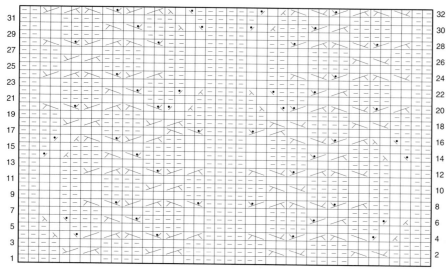

PRETZEL BRAID CHART

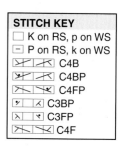

STITCH KEY

☐	K on RS, p on WS
−	P on RS, k on WS
⤬	C4B
⤬	C4BP
⤬	C4FP
	C3BP
	C3FP
⤬	C4F

RIB (AFTER CABLE)

RIB (BEFORE CABLE)

Row 17: Rep Row 1.

Row 18: Rep Row 2.

Row 19: Rep Row 1.

Row 20: P2, C4BP, C4FP, C4BP, C3FP, p6, C3BP, C4FP, C4BP, C4FP, p2.

Row 21: K2, p2, k4, p4, k3, p2, k6, p2, k3, p4, k4, p2, k2.

Row 22: P2, k2, p4, C4F, p3, C3FP, p4, C3BP, p3, C4F, p4, k2, p2.

Row 23: Rep Row 7.

Row 24: P2, C4FP, C4BP, C4FP, p2, k2, p4, k2, p2, C4BP, C4FP, C4BP, p2.

Row 25: K4, p4, k4, p2, k2, p2, k4, p2, k2, p2, k4, p4, k4.

Row 26: P4, C4B, p4, k2, p2, k2, p4, k2, p2, k2, p4, C4B, p4.

Row 27: Rep Row 25.

Row 28: P2, C4BP, C4FP, C4BP, p2, k2, p4, k2, p2, C4FP, C4BP, C4FP, p2.

Row 29: Rep Row 7.

Row 30: P2, k2, p4, C4F, p3, C3BP, p4, C3FP, p3, C4F, p4, k2, p2.

Row 31: K2, p2, k4, p4, k3, p2, k6, p2, k3, p4, k4, p2, k2.

Row 32: P2, C4FP, C4BP, C4FP, C3BP, p6, C3FP, C4BP, C4FP, C4BP, p2.

Rep Rows 1–32 for pat.

First Sleeve

Cast on 46 (50, 54) sts.

Row 1 (WS): Sel st, p2 (4, 6), work

Row 1 of cable pat over 40 sts, p2 (4, 6), sel st.

Work Row 2 as follows:

Small: Sel st, k2, work Row 2 of cable over 40 sts, k2, sel st.

Medium: Sel st, k1, p1, k2, work Row 2 of cable over 40 sts, k2, p1, k1, sel st.

Large: Sel st, [p1, k2] twice, work Row 2 of cable over 40 sts, [k2, p1] twice, sel st.

Continue in established pats, work M1 inc inside sel st on each side [every 4th row] 23 times, working new sts into rib pat. (92, 96, 100 sts)

Complete [32 rows of cable pat] 3 times for all sizes. (96 rows)

Body

Change to long circular needle to accommodate large number of sts. Do not join.

Cable cast on 55 (56, 57) sts for side seam. Work across new sts and 92 (96, 100) sleeve sts, turn. Cable cast on 55 (56, 57) sts for other side seam, work all new sts into rib pat and establish new sel sts. (202, 208, 214 sts)

Continue to work even and complete cable pat through Row 32. For size medium (large), rep Rows 1–8 (1–16).

Divide for neck

With WS facing, work across first 101

(104, 107) sts, join a 2nd ball of yarn and complete row.

Shape neck

With RS facing, work rib pat to within 3 sts of cable pat, k2tog, k1, work cable pat over next 19 sts, work last st on this side of neck as a sel st; on other side of neck, work first st as a sel st, work 19 sts in established cable, k1, ssk, complete row in rib pat.

Rep dec on each of next 2 RS rows. (98, 101, 104 sts on each side)

Work even, maintaining sel sts at bottom edge and each neck edge for 51 rows.

On Row 26 (2, 10) of cable pat, work inc on each side of neck opening: work rib pat to within 2 sts of cable pat, M1, k2, work established cable; on other side of neck, work established cable, k2, M1, complete row.

Rep inc on each of next 2 RS rows. (101, 104, 107 sts on each side)

Rejoin sides

With WS facing, work across all 202 (208, 214) sts in pat, working neck edge sel sts back into cable pat. For small this will be Row 1 of cable pat, medium Row 9, and large Row 17.

Work even on 202 (208, 214) sts through Row 32 of cable pat. For medium (large), rep Rows 1–16 (1–32) of cable pat.

Bind off for side seam

At beg of next 2 rows, bind off 55 (56, 57) sts for side seams.

Continue in pat on remaining 92 (96, 100) sts. Re-establish sel st on each edge of sleeve.

Second Sleeve

Working inside sel sts, dec 1 st on each side of sleeve [every 4th row] 23 times. Work even on 46 (50, 54) sts through Row 2 (18, 2) of cable pat. Bind off all sts.

Finishing

Fold sweater in half along top edge of sleeves and sew underarm and side seams.

Bottom trim

With circular needle and WS facing, pick up and k 1 st in each sel st. Purl 3 rnds, then bind off loosely in purl. ❖

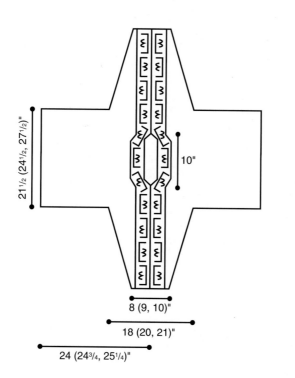

21½ (24½, 27½)"

10"

8 (9, 10)"

18 (20, 21)"

24 (24¾, 25¼)"

Pair of Sailing Pullovers

Designs by Kennita Tully

These smooth-sailing pullovers will shelter you and your little one from those cool ocean breezes. The unique design makes it easy to lengthen the sleeves for those children who are always growing.

Skill Level
Easy**

Size
Child's 4 (6, 8) and adult's small (medium, large, extra-large) Instructions are given for smallest size, with larger sizes in parentheses. Adult sizes follow in brackets. When only 1 number is given, it applies to all sizes.

Finished Measurements
Chest: 24 (28, 32) [36 (40, 44, 48)] inches

Length: 14 (15, 16) [20 (21, 21, 22)] inches

Materials
- Plymouth Fantasy Naturale worsted weight 100 percent mercerized cotton yarn (140 yds/100g per skein): child's sweater: 3 (3, 3, 4) skeins white #8001 (MC), 3 (3, 3, 4) skeins parakeet #2258 (CC); adult's sweater: 5 (5, 6, 7) skeins white #8001 (MC), 5 (5, 6, 7) skeins red #3611 (CC)
- Size 7 (4.5mm) 24-inch circular needle
- Size 8 (5mm) straight and 24-inch circular needles or size needed to obtain gauge
- Tapestry needle

Gauge
16 sts and 32 rows = 4 inches/10cm in garter st with larger needles

To save time, take time to check gauge.

Pattern Notes
Sweater is worked by knitting front and back center panels, then picking up sts along side of both panels and knitting to cuff.

Garter st is used throughout, alternating 2 rows of MC and 2 rows of CC.

Back Panel
With MC, cast on 24 (26, 28) [30 (32, 34, 36)] sts and work in garter st, alternating 2 rows MC and 2 rows CC until piece measures 13½ (14½, 15½) [19½ (20½, 20½, 21½)] inches. Bind off all sts.

Front Panel
Work as for back until piece measures 11 (12, 13) [17 (18, 18, 19)] inches.

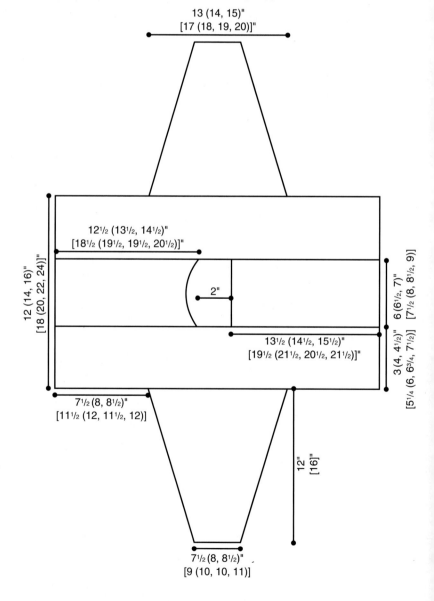

Shape neck

K7, attach new ball of yarn and bind off center 10 (12, 14) [16 (18, 20, 22)] sts, k last 7 sts. Working both sides at once with separate balls, dec 1 st at neck edge [every other row] 7 times. Fasten off.

Right Side

With CC and RS facing, pick up and

k 53 (57, 61) [77 (81, 81, 85)] sts along edge of back panel, cast on 8 sts, then pick up and k 51 (55, 59) [75 (79, 79, 83)] sts along left side of front panel. (112, 120, 128, [160, 168, 168, 176] sts)

Work even, alternating colors every 2 rows until piece measures 3 (4, 4½) [5¼ (6, 6¾, 7½)] inches.

Shape underarm

At beg of next 2 rows, bind off 30 (32, 34) [46 (48, 46, 48)] sts.

Shape sleeve

Working on remaining 52 (56, 60) [68 (72, 76, 80)] sts, dec 1 st at each side {every 10th (8th, 8th) [8th (8th, 6th, 6th) row} 4 (12, 9) [16 (16, 12, 12)] times, then {every 8th (0, 6th) [0 (0, 4th, 4th) row} 7 (0, 4) [0 (0, 6, 6)] times. (30, 32, 34, [36, 40, 40, 44] sts)

Change to smaller needles and work 2 more rows with CC. Bind off all sts.

Left Side

Work as for right side, pick up and k along edge of front panel, cast on 8 sts, then pick up and k along back panel.

Finishing

Wash and block to measurements.

With smaller needles and CC, pick up and k 48 (56, 64) [72 (80, 88, 96)] sts along front bottom edge. Work 2 rows CC, 2 rows MC, end with 3 rows CC. Bind off knitwise on WS. Rep for back bottom edge.

Sew sleeve and side seams.

Neck band

With smaller needles and maintaining color sequence, RS facing, pick up and k 24 (26, 28) [30 (32, 34, 36)] sts across back neck, 8 sts along cast on sts, 26 (28, 30) [32 (34, 36, 38)] sts across front neck, 8 sts along cast on sts. Do not join. (66, 70, 74, [78, 82, 86, 90] sts)

Work 2 rows CC, 2 rows MC, then 3 rows CC or 2 rows MC, 2 rows CC, 2 rows MC, 3 rows CC, depending on starting color. Bind off knitwise on WS with ending color. Seam ends of band. ❖

A Mountain Sojourn

Mountain Climber Pullover

Design by Dixie Butler

Worked in the round from the neck downward, the added texture of this pullover will hug your child with warmth during mountain-climbing adventures.

Skill Level
Intermediate***

Size
Child's 8 (10, 12) Instructions are given for smallest size, with larger sizes in parentheses. When only 1 number is given, it applies to all sizes.

Finished Measurements
Chest: 30 (32, 34) inches

Materials
- Plymouth Dreambaby DK 50 percent acrylic microfiber/50 percent nylon DK weight yarn (183 yds/50g per ball): 4 (5, 6) balls green #111
- Size 4 (3.5mm) double-pointed and 16-inch circular needles
- Size 6 (4.25mm) double-pointed, 16- and 24-inch circular needles
- Cable needle
- Stitch markers
- Stitch holders
- Tapestry needle

Gauge
20 sts and 34 rows = 4 inches/10cm in garter st

To save time, take time to check gauge.

Special Abbreviations
CF (Cable Front): Sl 3 sts to cn and hold in front, k3, k3 from cn.

CB (Cable Back): Sl 3 sts to cn and hold in back, k3, k3 from cn.

Pattern Stitch

Cable Panel (worked on 29 sts)
Row 1 and all unnumbered rows: P2, k6, p2, k9, p2, k6, p2.

Row 6: P2, k6, p2, k3, CB, p2, k6, p2.

Row 8: P2, CF, p2, k9, p2, CB, p2.

Row 12: P2, k6, p2, CF, k3, p2, k6, p2.

Row 16: P2, CF, p2, k9, p2, CB, p2.

Row 18: P2, k6, p2, k3, CB, p2, k6, p2.

Row 24: P2, CF, p2, CF, k3, p2, CB, p2.

Rep Rows 1–24 for pat.

Pattern Note
When working in the rnd, garter st is done by *knitting 1 rnd and purling 1 rnd. Rep from *.

Body
Beg at neck with smaller circular needle, cast on 78 (78, 78) sts. Pm between first and last st, join without twisting.

Work even in k1, p1 ribbing for 1½ inches.

Change to larger needle.

Set up pattern
Row 1: Inc 1 st in first st, k25, inc 1 st in next st, pm (back); inc 1 st in next st, k10, inc 1 st in next st, pm (sleeve); inc 1 st in next st, k6, p2, k9, p2, k6, inc 1 st (front); pm, inc 1 st in next st, k10, inc 1 st in next st, (sleeve). (29 sts each for front and back; 14 sts for each sleeve)

Rows 2 and 4: P to Cable Panel marker, p2, k6, p2, k9, p2, k6, p2, purl to end of rnd.

Row 3: Inc 1 st each side of every body marker as before, k to Cable Panel marker, p2, k6, p2, k9, p2, k6, p2, k to end of rnd. (94 sts)

Place additional markers on either side of front Cable Panel as sts are added to front.

Row 5: Inc 1 st each side of every body marker as before, k to Cable Panel marker p2, CF, p2, CF, k3, p2, CB, p2, k to end of rnd. (102 sts)

Beg with row 1 of Cable Panel pat, continue to inc 1 st each side of every body marker *at the same time* working body in garter st and Center Panel in established pat until there are 278 (294, 310) sts, ending with p row.

Divide for front, back & sleeves

Continuing in established pats and removing markers, k 77 (81, 85) sts for back, k 62 (66, 70) sts for left sleeve and sl to holder, k 77 (81, 85) sts for front, k 62 (66, 70) sts for right sleeve and sl to 2nd holder.

Replace marker so end of rnd is at right underarm.

Body

Continue in established pats on 154 (162, 170) body sts, work even until body measures 9 (9½, 10) inches from underarm, ending with a p row.

Ribbing

Change to smaller needles.

Work in k1, p1 ribbing, dec 14 (16, 18) sts evenly. (140, 146, 152 sts)

Work even in established pat until ribbing measures 2 inches.

Bind off.

Sleeves

Sl sts of 1 sleeve to larger dpn.

Join yarn at underarm,

pm between first and last st.

Row 1: Knit.

Rows 2 and 4: Purl.

Row 3: K1, k2tog, k to last 2 sts, ssk. [Rep these 4 rows] 9 times. (44, 48, 52 sts)

Work even in garter st until sleeve measures 9 (9½, 10) inches or desired length from underarm.

Cuff

Change to smaller dpn.

Work even in k1, p1 ribbing until cuff measures 2 inches.

Bind off. ❖

Camp Cables

Design by Diane Zangl

This rugged man's pullover is perfect for camping in the mountains.
It also has a most unusual starting point—the cable at the center of the chest.

Skill Level
Intermediate***

Size
Man's small (medium, large, extra-large) Instructions are given for smallest size, with larger sizes in parentheses. When only 1 number is given, it applies to all sizes.

Finished Measurements
Chest: 40 (44, 48, 52) inches
Armhole depth: 9 (9½, 10, 11) inches
Side to underarm: 16½ (17½, 18½, 19) inches
Sleeve length: 19 (20, 20½, 21) inches

Materials
- Plymouth Encore Heather 75 percent acrylic/25 percent wool worsted weight yarn (200 yds/ 100g per ball): 1 (1, 1, 2) balls brick #560 (A), 2 (2, 2, 3) balls putty #240 (B), 2 (3, 3, 4) balls spruce #668 (C), 2 (2, 3, 3) balls teal #670 (D)
- Size 4 (3.5mm) double-pointed, 16- and 24-inch circular needles
- Size 6 (4.25mm) double-pointed, 16- and 24-inch circular needles or size needed to obtain gauge
- Cable needle
- Stitch markers
- Stitch holders

Gauge
18 sts and 24 rows = 4 inches/10cm in St st on larger needles

To save time, take time to check gauge.

Special Abbreviations
FC (Front Cable—used on chest and right sleeve cap): Sl 3 sts to cn and hold in front, k3, k3 from cn.

BC (Back Cable—used on left sleeve

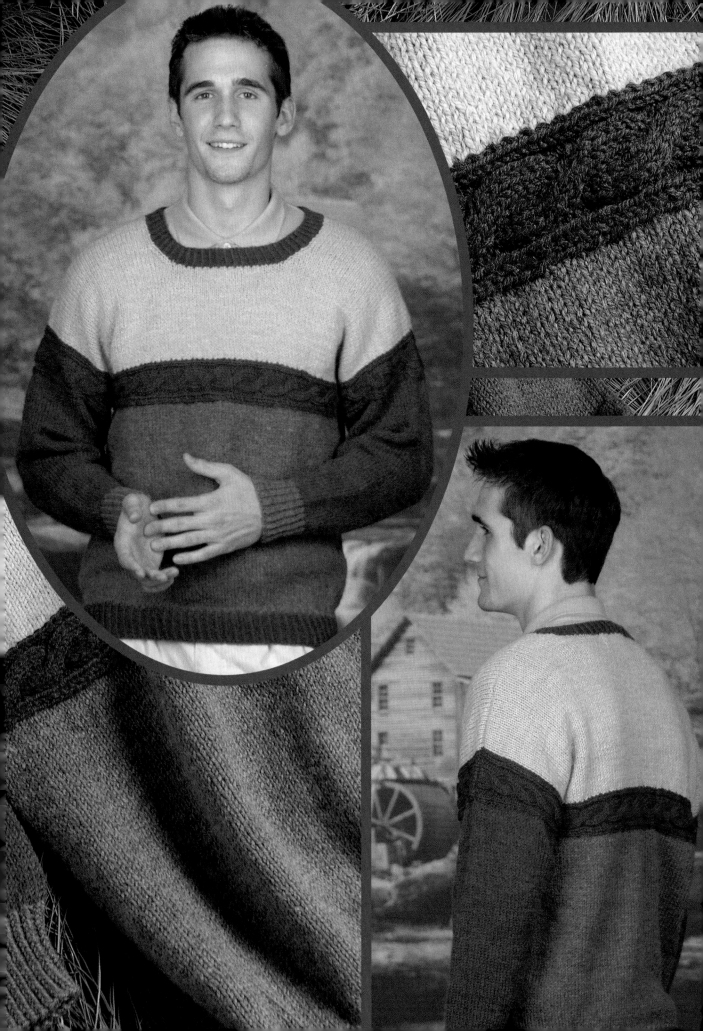

cap): Sl 3 sts to cn and hold in back, k3, k3 from cn.

Pattern Stitch

Cable Panel (worked on 14 sts)

Row 1 and all WS rows: P2, k2, p6, k2, p2.

Row 2: K2, p2, FC *or* BC, p2, k2.

Rows 4, 6, 8 and 10: K2, p2, k6, p2, k6.

Rep Rows 1–10 for pat.

Pattern Notes

A cable the length equal to the chest measurement is worked first, then sts are picked up and worked outwards from there, up for the yoke and down for the sleeves and lower body.

Cable crossings for sleeve caps are mirror images. Use Back Cable for left sleeve cap and Front Cable for right sleeve cap.

To avoid holes when changing colors, always bring new color up over old.

Body Cable

With A and larger needles, cast on 14 sts.

Work even in Cable Panel for approximately 40 (44, 48, 52) inches, ending with row 10 of pat. Bind off.

Sew bound-off edge to cast-on edge, forming a circle.

Mark seam st and at half-way point along both long edges for underarm.

Back Yoke & Sleeve Caps

With larger needles and A, cast on 14 sts, with B pick up and k 90 (99, 108, 117) sts between markers along 1 long edge, with 2nd ball of A cast on 14 sts. (118, 127, 136, 145 sts)

Keeping 14 sts at each end in mirror-image Cable Panels and remaining sts in St st, work even until armhole measures 9 (9½, 10, 11) inches, ending with a WS row.

Shape shoulders & back neck

Sl center 30 (33, 34, 37) sts to holder.

Working on both sides of neck with separate balls of yarn, bind off at each arm edge 14 sts once, then 10 (11, 12, 13) sts twice, and finally 10 (11, 13, 14) sts once.

Front Yoke & Sleeve Caps

With A pick up and k 1 st in each cast-on st of back sleeve cap, with B 90 (99, 108, 117) sts between markers of chest band, with A 14 sts along cast-on edge of 2nd sleeve cap.

Work as for back until armhole measures 5 (5½, 6, 7) inches, ending with a WS row.

Shape front neck

Sl center 22 (25, 26, 29) sts to holder. Working on both sides of neck with separate balls of yarn, [dec 1 st each side of neck every other row] 4 times.

Work even until armhole measures same as for back.

Shape shoulders as for back.

Sew shoulder seams.

Neck Band

With D and smaller 16-inch circular needle, k 30 (33, 34, 37) sts of back neck, pick up and k 30 sts along left side of neck, k 22 (25, 26, 29) sts of front neck, pick up and k 30 sts along right side of neck. (112, 118, 120, 126 sts)

Pm between first and last st.

Next rnd: *K1-tbl, p1, rep from * around.

Rep last rnd until neck band measures 1¼ (1¼, 1½, 1½) inches.

Bind off loosely in pat.

Body

With C and larger 24-inch circular needle, [pick up and k 90 (99, 108, 117) sts between markers on remaining long edge of chest cable] twice. (180, 198, 216, 234 sts)

Pm between first and last st.

Work even in St st until body measures 14 (15, 15½, 16) inches including chest cable, dec 26 (30, 32, 36) sts evenly on last rnd. (154, 168, 184, 198 sts)

Lower Band

Change to D and smaller needles.

Work in rib as for neck band until lower band measures 2½ (2½, 3, 3) inches.

Bind off loosely in pat.

Sleeves

Beg at underarm with D and larger 16-inch circular needle, pick up and k 81 (87, 91, 99) sts around arm cable.

Mark underarm st. Work even for 2 inches.

[Dec 1 st each side of marker every 4th rnd] 19 (21, 22, 25) times, changing to dpn when necessary. (43, 45, 47, 49) sts.

Cuff

Change to C and smaller needles.

Knit 1 rnd, dec 3 sts evenly. (40, 42, 44, 46 sts)

Work even in ribbing as for neck band until cuff measures 3 inches.

Bind off loosely in pat. ❖

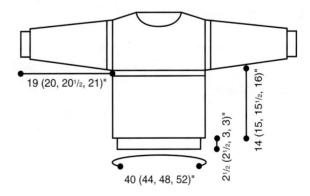

Homage to Horst

Design by Barbara Venishnick

This pullover is worked in strips that are joined as they are knit using a special technique developed by Horst Schulz and described in his book Patchwork Knitting. *This method allows the use of color in vertical sections without the use of bobbins.*

Skill Level
Advanced****

Size
Adult small (medium, large, extra-large) Instructions are given for smallest size, with larger sizes in parentheses. When only 1 number is given, it applies to all sizes.

Finished Measurements
Chest: 42 (45, 48, 51) inches
Finished length: 22 (23, 24, 25) inches

Materials
- Plymouth Indiecita worsted weight 100 percent Peruvian alpaca yarn (100 yds/50g per ball): 12 (13, 13, 14) balls camel #206 (A), 4 (5, 5, 6) balls Aran #100 (B)
- Size 6 (4.25mm) double-pointed, 16- and 29-inch circular needles or size needed to obtain gauge
- Cable needle
- Stitch markers
- Stitch holders

Gauge
16 sts and 34 rows = 4 inches/10cm in garter st
To save time, take time to check gauge.

Special Abbreviation
Slb: Sl 1 with yarn in back.
Slf: Sl 1 with yarn in front.
C3B: Sl 3 to cn, hold in back, k3, k3 from cn.
C3F: Sl 3 to cn, hold in front, k3, k3 from cn.
K1b: Knit 1 through the back loop.

Pattern Notes
Each body strip is worked in a particular order, from left to right, beg at outer edge of back left shoulder. See Chart A for order of construction.

Sleeves are worked in strips from armhole to cuff. See Chart B for order of strips.

Sleeve cables are worked in reverse order from body cable. Because it is knit "upside down," working in this fashion makes the cables in the sleeve and body of the finished sweater appear the same.

Body

Strip 1
With A and 1 dpn, cast on 15 sts.
Row 1 (RS): K1b, p2, k9, p2, slf.
Row 2: K1b, k2, p9, k2, slf.
Row 3: K1b, p2, C3B, k3, p2, slf.
Row 4: Rep Row 2.
Row 5: Rep Row 1.
Row 6: Rep Row 2.
Row 7: K1b, p2, k3, C3F, p2, slf.
Row 8: Rep Row 2.
Rep Rows 1–8 until first strip is 21 (22, 23, 24) inches long.
Sl all sts to small holder.

Strip 2
With A and 2 dpns held tog, cast on 9 (10, 11, 12) sts. Remove 1 needle.
Row 1 (RS): With B, k1b, k7 (8, 9, 10), slb, holding first strip parallel to 2nd strip, pick up 1 st in first edge st at bottom right side of first strip, psso, turn.
Row 2: With B, slf, k7 (8, 9, 10), slf.
Row 3: With A, k1b, k7 (8, 9, 10), slb, pick up 1 st in next edge st of first strip, psso, turn.
Row 4: With A, rep Row 2.

Rep Rows 1–4 until all edge sts of strip 1 are used.
Work 2 more rows with color that is next in sequence as follows:
Row 1: K1b, k7 (8, 9, 10), slf.
Row 2: K1b, k7 (8, 9, 10), slf.
Sl all sts to small holder.

Strip 3
With A and 1 dpn, cast on 15 sts.
Row 1 (RS): K1b, p2, k9, p2, slb, hold finished strips parallel with strip 3, pick up 1 st in first edge st at lower right of strip 2, psso, turn.
Row 2: K1b, k2, p9, k2, slf.
Row 3: K1b, p2, C3B, k3, slb, pick up 1 st in next edge st of strip 2, psso.
Row 4: Rep Row 2.
Row 5: Rep Row 1.
Row 6: Rep Row 2.
Row 7: K1b, p2, k3, C3F, p2, slb, pick up 1 st in next edge st of strip 2, psso.
Row 8: Rep Row 2.
Rep Rows 1–8 until all edge sts of strip 2 are used.
Work 2 more rows in the manner of strip 1.
Sl all sts to small holder.

Strip 4
Work as for strip 2, making this strip 2 rows longer than strip 3.
Sl all sts to small holder.

Strip 5
Work as for strip 3 until all edge sts of strip 4 are worked.
Place sts on st holder; do not add any extra rows.

Strip 6
Work as for strip 2, working to same length as strip 5.

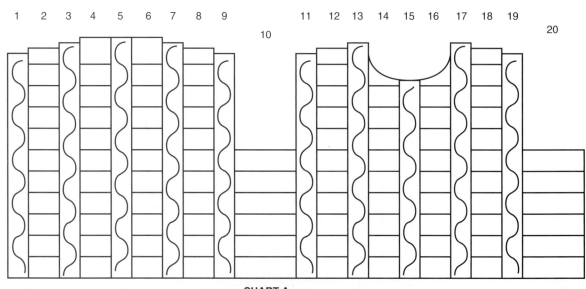

CHART A
CONSTRUCTION ORDER
FRONT & BACK

Place sts on holder.

Strip 7

Work as for strip 3, working until all but 1 of the edge sts of strip 6 are used, and making this strip 2 rows shorter than the 1 before.

Strip 8

Work as for strip 2, working until all but 1 of the edge sts of strip 7 are used, and making this strip 2 rows shorter than the 1 before.

Strip 9

Work as for strip 3, working until all but 1 of the edge sts of strip 8 are used, and making this strip 2 rows shorter than the 1 before.

Strip 10

With A and 2 dpns held tog, cast on 18 (20, 22, 24) sts. Remove 1 needle.

Row 1 (RS): With B, k1b, k16 (18, 20, 22), slb, pick up 1 st in first edge st of strip 9, psso, turn.

Row 2: With B, slf, k16 (18, 20, 22) slf.

Row 3: With A, rep Row 1.

Row 4: With A, rep Row 2.

Rep Rows 1–4 until this underarm section is 12 (12½, 13, 13½) inches from cast-on edge.

Bind off all sts loosely.

Strip 11

Work as for strip 3. When all edge sts

of strip 10 are used, continue as for strip 1, making strip 11 equal in length to strip 9.

Place sts on holder.

Strip 12

Work as for strip 2. When all edge sts of strip 11 are used, work an additional 2 rows.

Strip 13

Work as for strip 2. When all edge sts of strip 12 are used, work an additional 2 rows.

Strip 14

Work as for strip 2 until 3½ inches shorter than strip 13.

Beg neck shaping

Continue colors in established sequence.

Row 1 (RS): K4 (5, 6, 7) and place on holder for front neck, k4, slb, pick up 1 in next edge st of strip 13, psso, turn.

Row 2: Slf, k4.

Row 3: K1, ssk, k1, slb, pick up 1, psso.

Row 4: Slf, k3.

Row 5: K1, ssk, slb, pick up 1, psso.

Row 6: Slf, k2.

Row 7: Ssk, slf, pick up 1, psso.

Row 8: Slf, k1.

Row 9: Ssk, pull yarn through last loop, cut yarn.

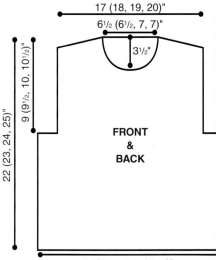

Strip 15

Work as for strip 3, working until even with sts on front neck holder.

Strip 16

Work as for strip 2 until all edge sts of strip 15 are used.

Beg neck shaping

Continue colors in established sequence.

Row 1 (RS): K1b, k4, place remaining 4 (5, 6, 7) sts on holder for front neck.

Row 2: K4, slf.

Row 3: K1b, k2tog, k2.

Row 4: K3, slf.

Row 5: K1b, k2tog, k1.

Row 6: K2, slf.

Row 7: K1b, k2tog.

Row 8: K1, slf.

Row 9: K2tog, pull yarn through last loop, cut yarn.

Strip 17

Work as for strip 3 until all edge sts of strip 16 are used.

Continue as for strip 1 until this strip is the same length as strip 13.

Place sts on holder.

Strip 18

Work as for strip 2 until this strip is 2 rows shorter than strip 17.

Place sts on holder.

Strip 19

Work as for strip 3 until this strip is 2 rows shorter than strip 18.

Strip 20

Work as for strip 10.

Join Strips to Form Body

With work inside out, form a circle and place strip 1 next to strip 20.

Sew tog on inside. This creates a ridge on RS of work similar to the one formed by knitted-in joining method.

Shoulder Seams

With work still inside out, working left and right shoulders separately, return front sts to needle, return back sts to a 2nd needle.

With 3rd needle, bind off loosely using 3-needle bind off.

Leave front and back neck sts on holders.

Turn sweater right side out.

Sleeves

With RS facing using A and longer circular needle, pick up and k 79 (82, 85, 88) sts evenly spaced in edge sts of armhole.

Pm on either side of center 9 (10, 11, 12) sts. These should be centered on the shoulder seam.

Count 9 sts out on either side of these center sts and pm in these positions as well. Turn.

With short needle and A, k 25 (26, 27, 28) sts, slf, leave remaining 53 (55, 57, 59) sts on circular needle. Hold sts in place with stoppers.

Sleeve Strip 1

Row 1 (RS): With B, k1b, k23 (24, 25, 26), slf.

Row 2: With B, k1b, k23 (24, 25, 26), slf.

Row 3: With A, rep Row 1.

Row 4: With A, rep Row 2.

Rep Rows 1–4 once more.

Dec row (RS): With B, k1b, knit to last 3 sts, k2tog, slf.

Continue in color sequence as established [working dec row every 8th row] 17 more times. (8, 9, 10, 11 sts)

Work 7 more rows even.

Place sts on holder.

Sleeve Strip 2

With A and WS facing, working with 9 sts between first set of markers, knit across inc 6 sts evenly spaced. (15 sts)

Work cable

Row 1 (RS): K1b, p2, k9, p2, slb, pick up 1, psso.

Row 2: Slf, k2, p9, k2, slf.

Row 3: K1b, p2, C3F, k3, p2, slb, pick up 1, psso.

Row 4: Slf, k2, p9, k2, slf.

Row 5: K1b, p2, k9, p2, slb, pick up 1, psso.

Row 6: Slf, k2, p9, k2, slf.

Row 7: K1b, p2, k3, C3B, p2, slb, pick up 1, psso.

Row 8: Slf, k2, p9, k2, slf.

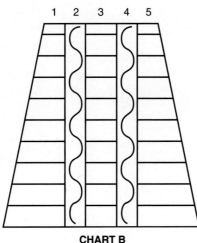

CHART B
CONSTRUCTION ORDER
SLEEVE

Rep Rows 1–8 until all the edge sts of strip 1 have been used.

Place all sts on holder.

Sleeve Strip 3

With A and WS facing, k 9 (10, 11, 12) sts between markers at top of shoulder.

Leave remaining 35 (36, 37, 38) sts on circular needle with stoppers.

Work as for strip 2 of body until all edge sts of sleeve strip 2 are used.

Place sts on holder.

Sleeve Strip 4

Work as for sleeve strip 2.

Sleeve Strip 5

With A and WS facing, k 26 (27, 28, 29) sts from circular needle.

Work even as for strip 3 in same color sequence for 8 rows.

Dec row: K1b, k2tog, knit to within 1 st of end of strip, slb, pick up 1 st, psso.

Continue in color sequence as established, [working dec row every 8th row] 17 more times.

Work even on 8 (9, 10, 11) sts until all edge sts of strip 4 are used.

Place sts on holder.

Sleeve Cuff

Place all sleeve sts on needle.

With A and RS facing, k 8 (9, 10, 11) sts of strip 5, dec 6 sts evenly over 15 sts of strip 4, k 9 (10, 11, 12) sts of strip 3, dec 6 sts evenly over 15 sts of strip 2, k 8 (9, 10, 11) sts of strip 1. (43, 46, 49, 52 sts)

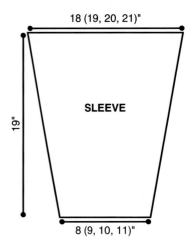

18 (19, 20, 21)"

SLEEVE

19"

8 (9, 10, 11)"

Work even in St st for 4 rows.

Bind loosely on WS purlwise.

Underarm Seams

Sew half of bound-off sts at top of strips 10 and 20 to side of sleeve.

Sew the other half of bound-off sts to other side of sleeve.

Sew remaining underarm seam, with RS out in usual way.

Bottom Edge

With RS facing, using A and large circular needle, pick up and k 7 sts along bottom edge of each cable strip, and 1 st in each cast-on st of the stripe strips.

Knit 4 rounds.

Bind off loosely knitwise, allowing bottom trim to roll.

Neck Band

Beg at the top of strip 6 with RS facing and A, k 9 (10, 11, 12) sts of strip 6; on strip 5 [k2tog] 6 times, k3tog; k 9 (10, 11, 12) sts of strip 4; pick up and k 13 sts along left side of neck; k 4 (5, 6, 7) sts of strip 16; on strip 15 [k2tog] 6 times, k3tog; k 4 (5, 6, 7) sts of strip 14; pick up and k 13 sts along right side of neck. (66, 70, 74, 78 sts)

Join and mark for beg of rnd.

Purl 1 rnd with A.

*With B, knit 1 rnd, purl 1 rnd. With A, knit 1 rnd, purl 1 rnd.

Rep from * once.

Facing

With A, knit 9 rnds.

Bind off loosely knitwise.

Fold facing to inside and sew in place. ❖

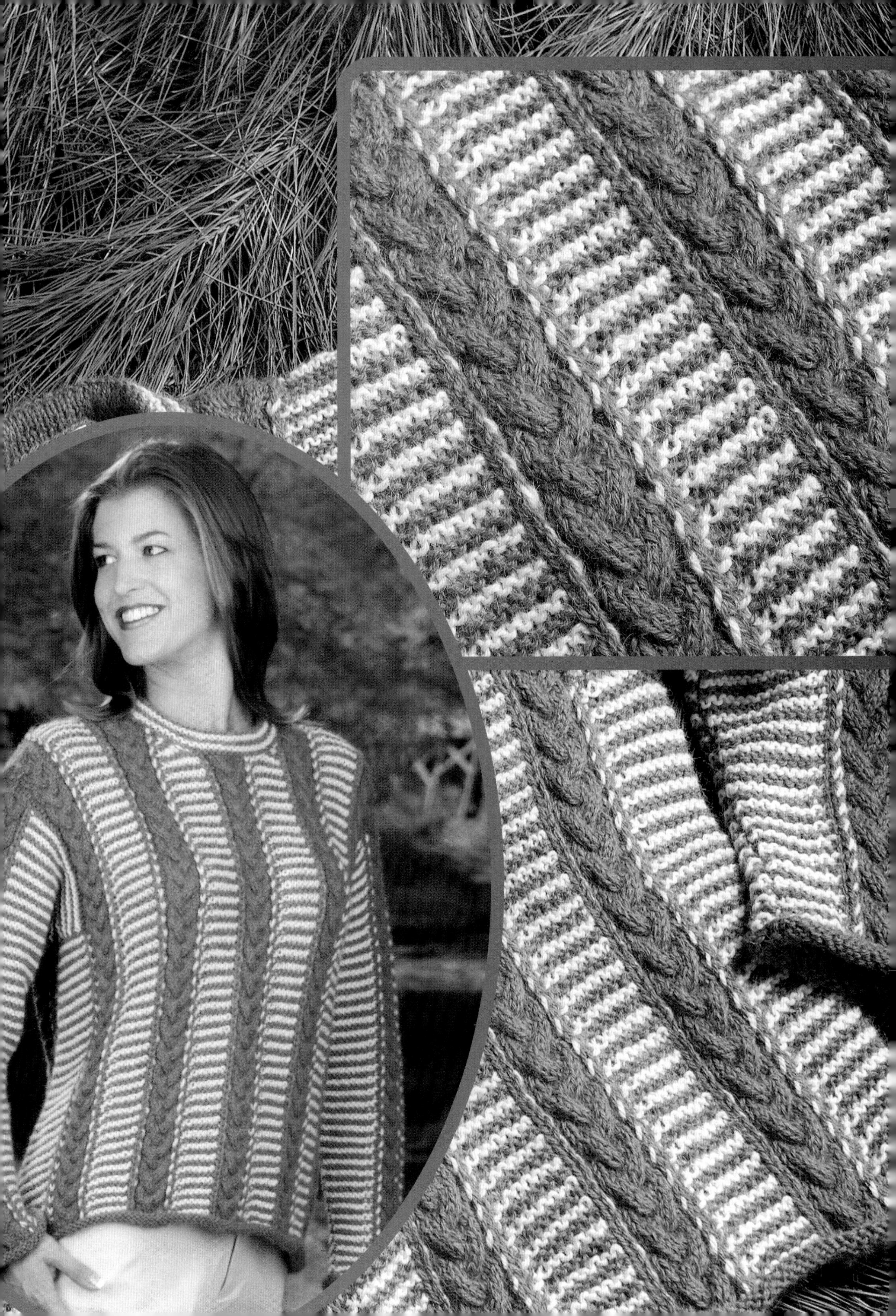

Adirondack Weekend

Design by Kathy Sasser

A trip to the Adirondack Mountains in New York is certainly a memory-maker for all. Recapture that special time with this picturesque man's sweater.

Skill Level
Advanced****

Size
Man's small (medium, large)
Instructions are given for smallest size, with larger sizes in parentheses. When only 1 number is given, it applies to all sizes.

Finished Measurements
Chest: 38 (42, 46) inches
Sleeve length: 20 inches
Total length: 25 (26½, 28) inches

Materials
- Plymouth's Encore DK weight 75 percent acrylic/25 percent wool (150 yds/50g per ball): 8 (9, 9) balls dark green #204 (MC), 3 balls soft white #146, 1 ball each gold #1014, light green #054, brown tweed #7172, red #9601, dark blue #517, light blue #515, black #217 and bone tweed #7357
- Size 3 (3.25mm) 16- and 24-inch circular needles
- Size 5 (3.75mm) 24-inch circular needle or size needed to obtain gauge
- Stitch holder
- Stitch markers
- Tapestry needle

Gauge
24 sts and 32 rows = 4 inches/10cm in St st with larger needles

To save time, take time to check gauge.

Pattern Notes
The front of sweater is worked first. The back progresses from the front shoulders and is worked from the top down.

When working front chart, read all odd-numbered (RS) rows from right to left and all even-numbered (WS) from left to right.

When working sleeve charts, odd-numbered rows become WS rows and are read left to right. Even-numbered rows are RS rows and are read right to left.

Smaller designs can be worked successfully using duplicate st, while larger areas can be worked using the Intarsia method.

Front
With smaller needles and MC, cast on 106 (116, 126) sts. Work even in k1, p1 rib for 2½ inches, inc 10 (12, 14) sts evenly across last WS row. (116, 128, 140 sts)

Change to larger needles and St st.

Referring to front chart in chosen size, work even until neck shaping is reached, pm at each side as indicated for underarm.

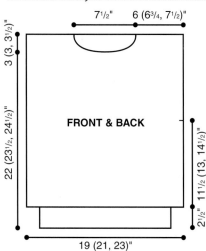

7½" 6 (6¾, 7½)"

3 (3, 3½)"

FRONT & BACK

22 (23½, 24½)"

11½ (13, 14½)"

2½"

19 (21, 23)"

Sl center 24 (28, 26) sts for front neck to holder and dec for neck shaping as indicated.

Complete front chart through row 180 (192, 204). Do not bind off.

Back

Next row (RS): With MC, k across 37 (41, 46) shoulder sts, on same needle cast on 42 (46, 48) sts, then k across remaining 37 (41, 46) sts. (116, 128, 140 sts)

Work even in St st until 89 rows have been completed, mark each end for underarm.

Continue until 180 (192, 204) rows have been completed.

Ribbing

Next row (RS): Change to smaller needles and knit 1 row, dec 10 (12, 14) sts evenly across. (106, 116, 126 sts)

Work even in k1, p1 rib for 2½ inches.

Bind off loosely.

Neck Band

With 16-inch circular needle and MC pick up and k 23 (23, 27) sts down

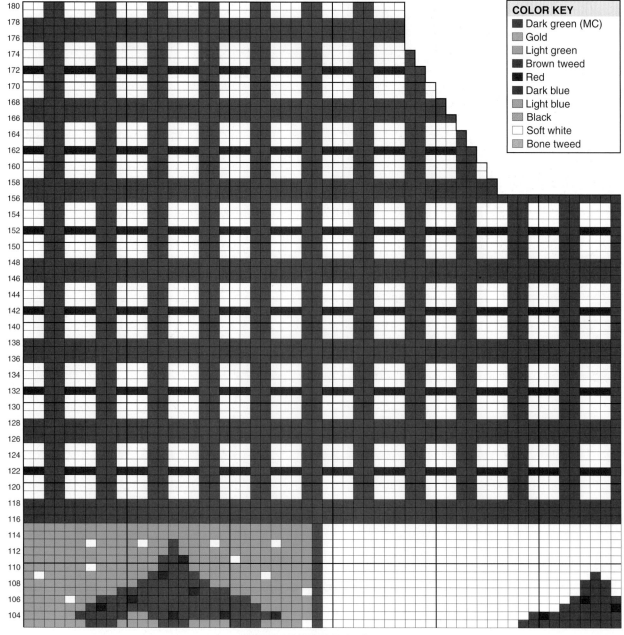

COLOR KEY
- Dark green (MC)
- Gold
- Light green
- Brown tweed
- Red
- Dark blue
- Light blue
- Black
- Soft white
- Bone tweed

FRONT CHART SIZE S TOP LEFT

left side of neck, k across center 24 (28, 26) sts, pick up and k 23 (23, 27) sts along right side of neck, k across center back 42 (46, 48) sts. (112, 120, 128 sts)

Pm between first and last st, work in k1, p1 rib for 3¼ inches.

Bind off loosely.

Fold neck band in half to inside and st in place.

Sleeves

With RS facing, using larger needles and MC, pick up and k 132 sts

between markers on sweater front and back.

Follow appropriate chart for left or right sleeve beg with row 1, making decs as indicated and working through row 132. (60 sts)

Change to smaller needles.

With MC, purl 1 row dec 6 sts evenly. (54 sts)

Work in k1, p1 rib for 2½ inches.

Bind off loosely.

Finishing

Sew side and underarm seams. ❖

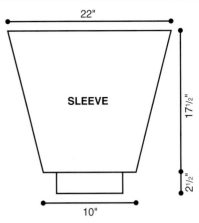

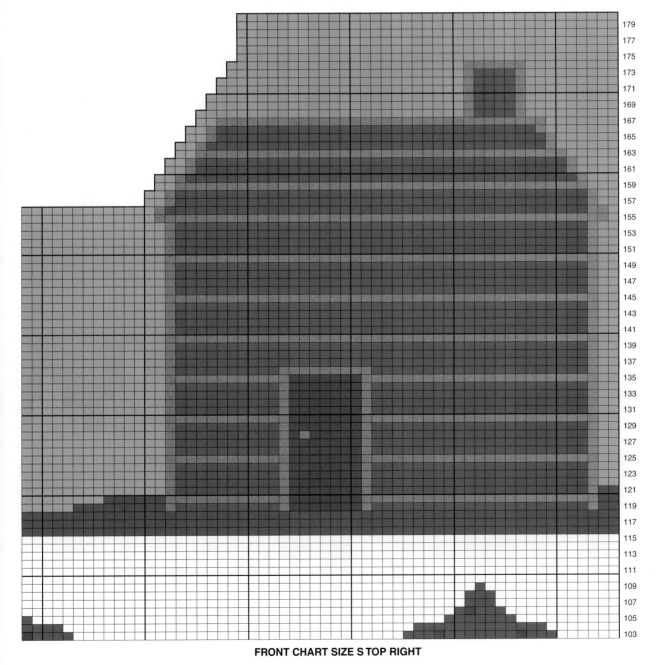

FRONT CHART SIZE S TOP RIGHT

FRONT CHART SIZE S BOTTOM LEFT

FRONT CHART SIZE S BOTTOM RIGHT

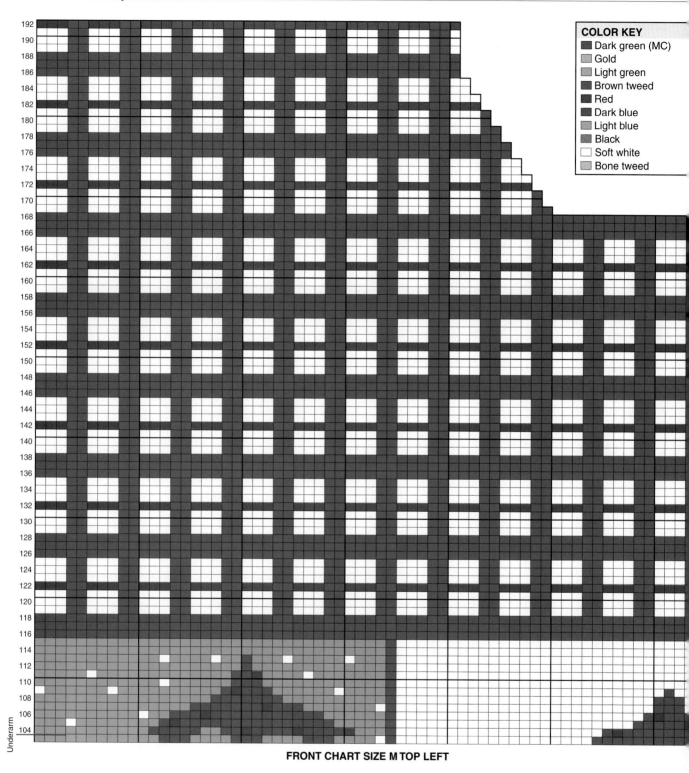

COLOR KEY
- Dark green (MC)
- Gold
- Light green
- Brown tweed
- Red
- Dark blue
- Light blue
- Black
- Soft white
- Bone tweed

Underarm

FRONT CHART SIZE M TOP LEFT

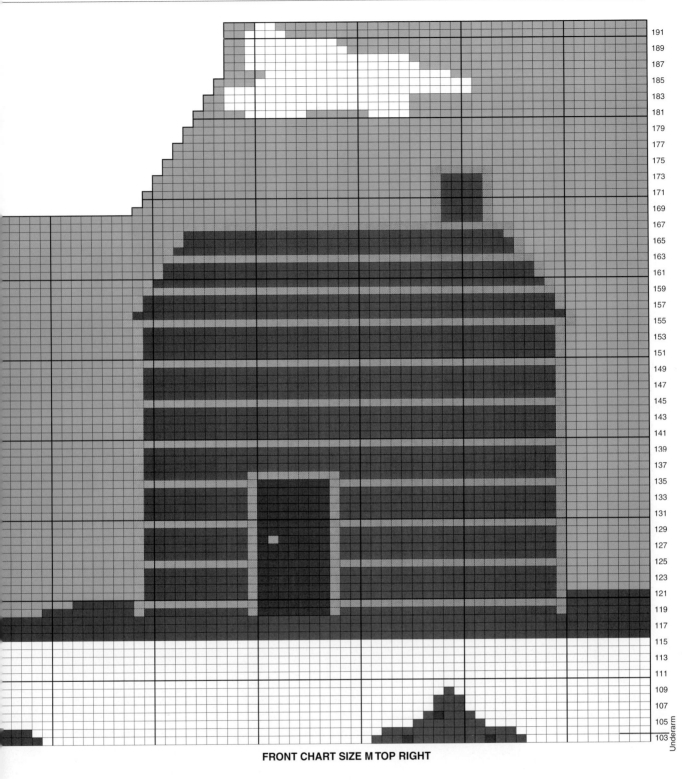

191
189
187
185
183
181
179
177
175
173
171
169
167
165
163
161
159
157
155
153
151
149
147
145
143
141
139
137
135
133
131
129
127
125
123
121
119
117
115
113
111
109
107
105
103

Underarm

FRONT CHART SIZE M TOP RIGHT

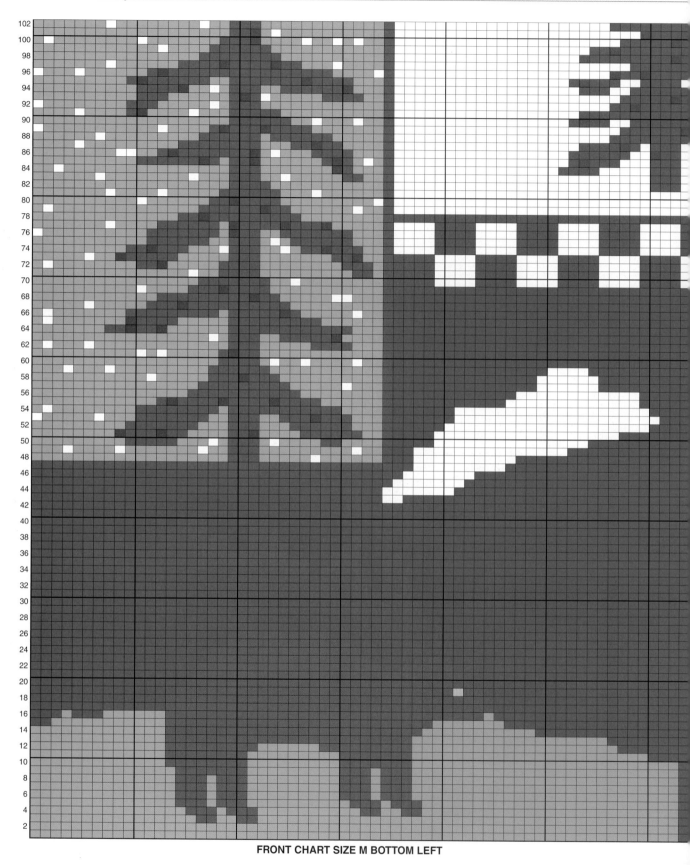

FRONT CHART SIZE M BOTTOM LEFT

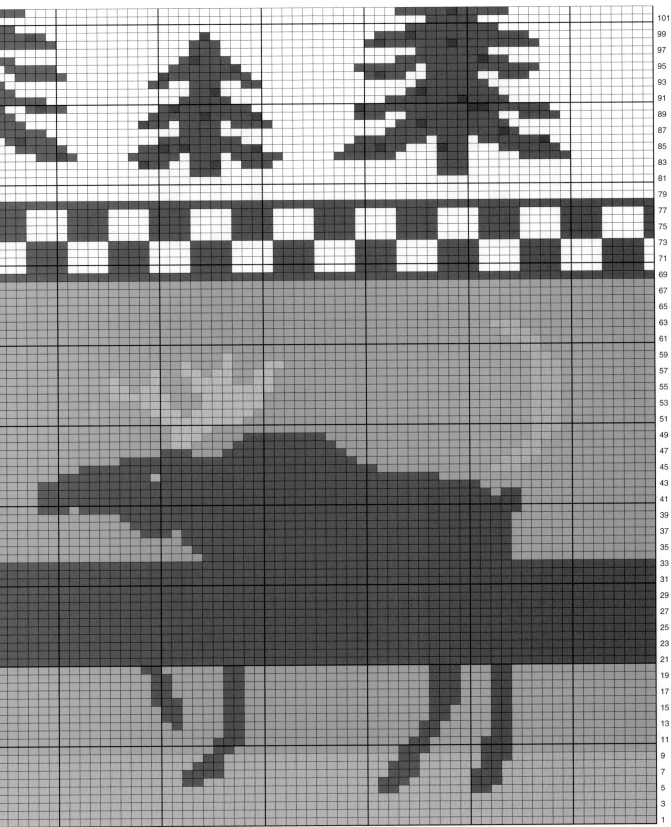

FRONT CHART SIZE M BOTTOM RIGHT

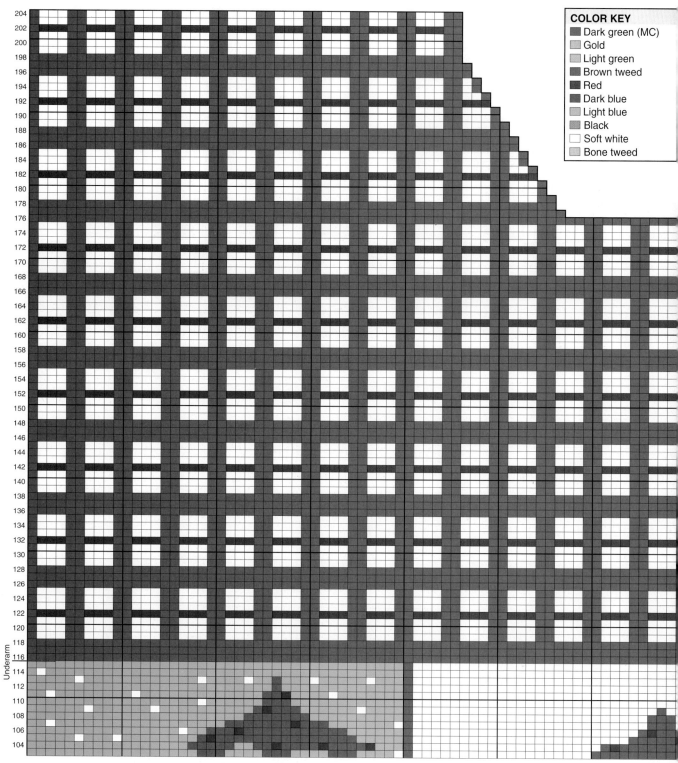

COLOR KEY
- Dark green (MC)
- Gold
- Light green
- Brown tweed
- Red
- Dark blue
- Light blue
- Black
- Soft white
- Bone tweed

FRONT CHART SIZE L TOP LEFT

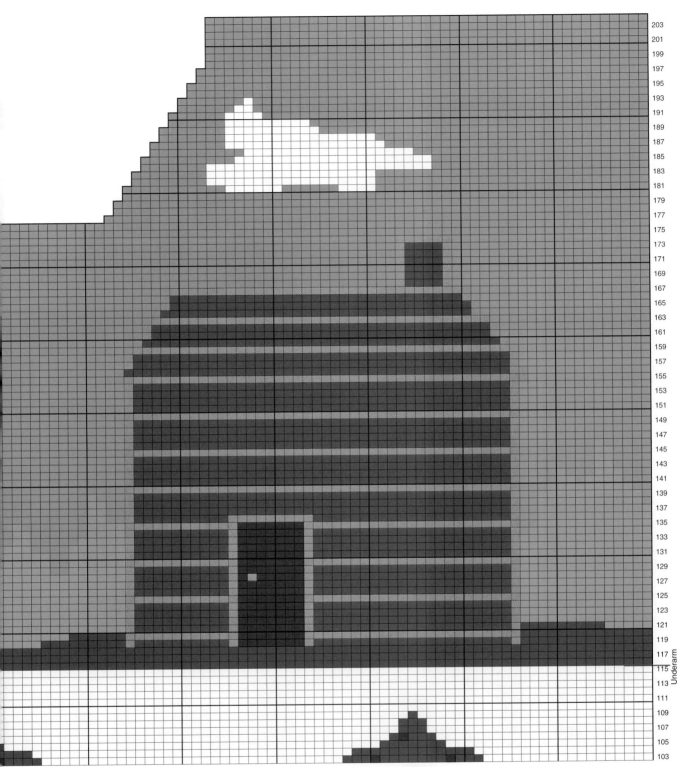

203
201
199
197
195
193
191
189
187
185
183
181
179
177
175
173
171
169
167
165
163
161
159
157
155
153
151
149
147
145
143
141
139
137
135
133
131
129
127
125
123
121
119
117
115 Underarm
113
111
109
107
105
103

FRONT CHART SIZE L TOP RIGHT

FRONT CHART SIZE L BOTTOM LEFT

FRONT CHART SIZE L BOTTOM RIGHT

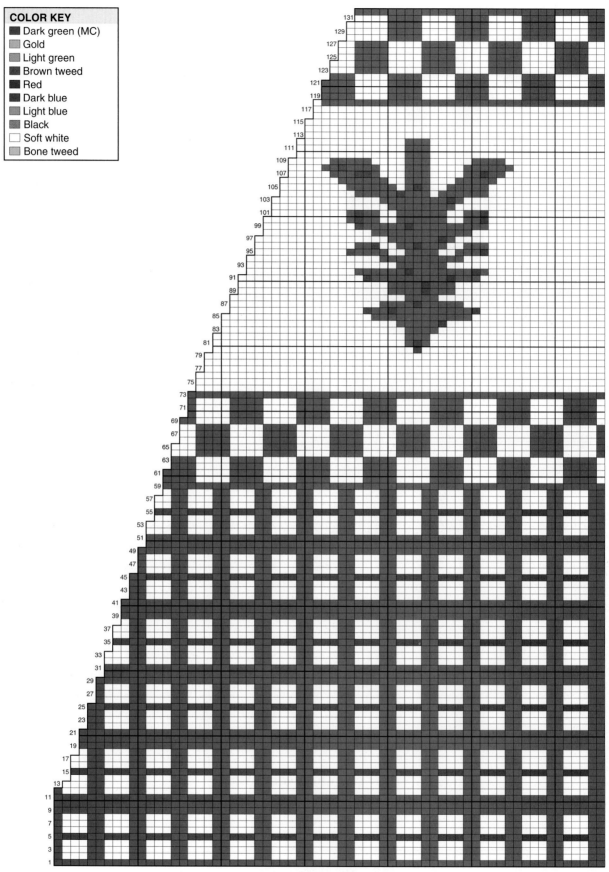

COLOR KEY
- ■ Dark green (MC)
- ▨ Gold
- ▨ Light green
- ▨ Brown tweed
- ■ Red
- ■ Dark blue
- ▨ Light blue
- ▨ Black
- □ Soft white
- ▨ Bone tweed

LEFT SIDE OF LEFT SLEEVE
ALL SIZES

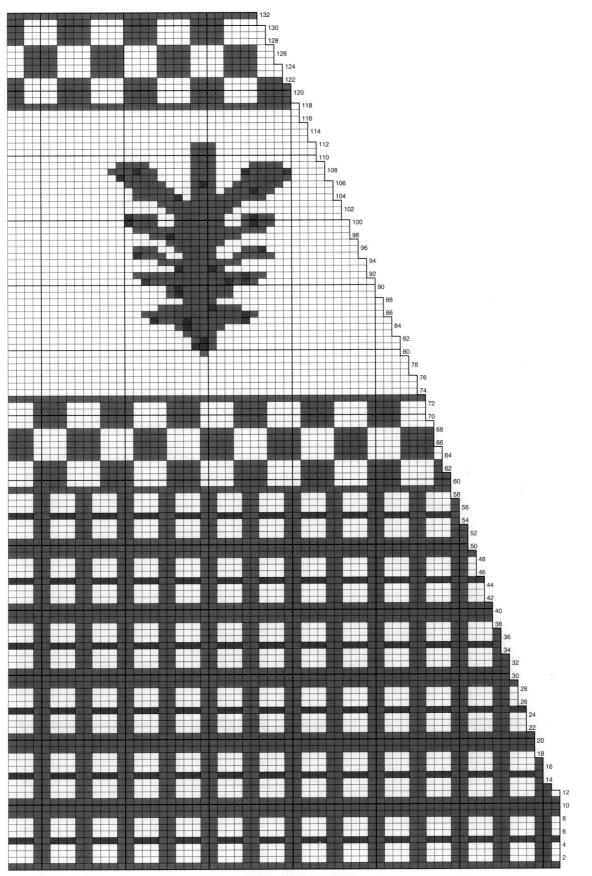

RIGHT SIDE OF LEFT SLEEVE
ALL SIZES

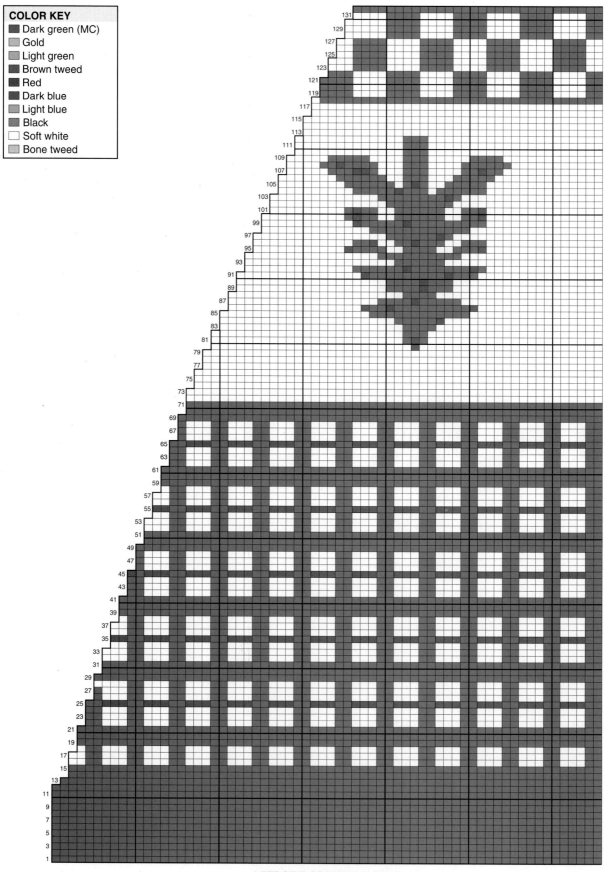

COLOR KEY
- ■ Dark green (MC)
- □ Gold
- ▨ Light green
- ■ Brown tweed
- ■ Red
- ■ Dark blue
- ▨ Light blue
- ■ Black
- □ Soft white
- ▨ Bone tweed

LEFT SIDE OF RIGHT SLEEVE
ALL SIZES

RIGHT SIDE OF RIGHT SLEEVE
ALL SIZES

Mountain Greenery

Design by Lois S. Young

This sweater is perfect for a refreshing hike through the pines. The wave pattern of the lower body is reminiscent of a mountain stream.

Skill Level

Intermediate***

Size

Woman's small (medium, large, extra-large) Instructions are given for smallest size, with larger sizes in parentheses. When only 1 number is given, it applies to all sizes.

Finished Measurements

Chest: 34 (38, 42½, 46¾) inches
Length: 23½ (25, 26½, 28) inches

Materials

- Plymouth Encore worsted weight 75 percent acrylic/25 percent wool yarn (200 yds/100g per skein): 4 (4, 5, 6) skeins light sage #1231 (MC), 2 (2, 2, 3) skeins medium sage #1232 (CC)
- Size 6 (4.25mm) straight and 16-inch circular needle
- Size 7 (4.5mm) straight and 16-inch circular needle or size needed to obtain gauge
- 3 (⅝-inch) buttons, La Mode Ox Silver #2412
- Stitch holders
- Stitch markers

Gauge

18 sts and 24 rows = 4 inches/10cm in Lower Body pat with larger needles

19 sts and 25 rows = 4 inches/10cm in St st with larger needles

To save time, take time to check gauge.

Pattern Stitches

Lower Body (sizes small and large only)

Rows 1, 3, 5, 7 and 9: Sl 1, k7, *k1, [k2tog] twice, [yo, k1] 3 times, yo, [ssk] twice, rep from * across, end last rep k9.

Rows 2 and 10: Sl 1, k to end of row.

Rows 4, 6 and 8: Sl 1, k7, p to last 8 sts, k8.

Rep Rows 1–10 in sequence of 10 rows CC, 10 rows MC.

Lower Body (sizes medium and extra-large only)

Rows 1, 3, 5, 7 and 9: Sl 1, k7, *k1, [k2tog] twice, [yo, k1] 3 times, yo, [ssk] twice, rep from * across, end last rep k1, [k2tog] twice, [yo, k1] twice, k8.

Rows 2 and 10: Sl 1, k to end of row.

Rows 4, 6 and 8: Sl 1, k7, p to last 8 sts, k8.

Rep Rows 1–10 in sequence of 10 rows CC, 10 rows MC.

Pattern Notes

For Lower Body pat, first st of each row is slipped purlwise to form chained edge.

For easier seaming, work neck and underarm decreases on 2nd and 3rd sts from the edge.

For sizes medium and extra-large, lower body piece should be positioned so a whole scallop is on top and a half scallop is at the bottom.

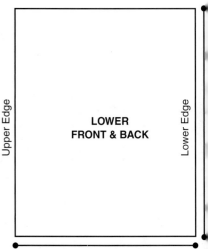

LOWER
FRONT & BACK

Upper Edge

Lower Edge

14 (15, 16, 17)"

Lower Body Panels
Make 2

With larger needle and CC, cast on 65 (71, 77, 83) sts. Knit 1 row.

Beg with Row 2 of Lower Body pat, work even until there are 10 (11, 12, 13) stripes.

Bind off all sts.

Back Yoke

With RS facing using smaller needles and CC, beg with 9th (10th, 11th, 12th) chained edge st, pick up and k 67 (75, 79, 85) sts evenly spaced

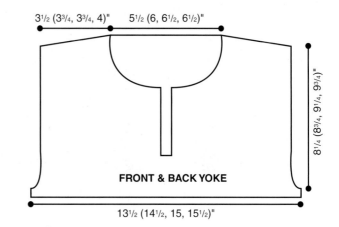

3½ (3¾, 3¾, 4)"   5½ (6, 6½, 6½)"

8¼ (8¾, 9¼, 9¾)"

FRONT & BACK YOKE

13½ (14½, 15, 15½)"

across top of back, leaving 8 (9, 10, 11) edge sts unworked.

Knit 3 rows.

Change to larger needles and MC.

Working in St st, [dec 1 st each end every RS row] 4 (5, 6, 7) times. (59, 65, 67, 71 sts)

Work even until armhole measures 8½ (8¾, 9¼, 9¾) inches.

Shape shoulders

Bind off 7 (8, 8, 9) sts at beg of next 2 rows, then 8 (8, 9, 9) sts at beg of following 2 rows.

Sl remaining 29 (31, 33, 35) sts to holder for back neck.

Front Yoke

Work as for back until armhole measures 1½ inches, ending with a WS row.

K 28 (30, 32, 34) sts for left side of neck and sl to holder, bind off 3 sts for neck placket, k to end of row.

Work even on right side of neck until armhole measures 7 (7½, 8, 8½) inches, ending with a WS row.

Shape neckline

K 9 (10, 11, 12) sts for neck and sl to holder, k to end of row. (19, 20, 21, 22 sts)

[Dec 1 st at neck edge every RS row] 4 times. (15, 16, 17, 18 sts)

Work even until armhole measures same as for back.

Shape shoulders

Bind off at arm edge 7 (8, 8, 9) sts once, then 8 (8, 9, 9) sts once.

Sl sts of left side of neck from holder to needle. Work as for right side, reversing shaping.

Sew shoulder seams.

Sleeves

With RS facing using smaller

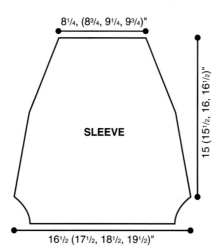

8¼, (8¾, 9¼, 9¾)"

15 (15½, 16, 16½)"

SLEEVE

16½ (17½, 18½, 19½)"

16-inch circular needle and CC, pick up and k 8 (9, 10, 11) sts along underarm, pm, 6 (7, 8, 9) sts along dec area of armhole, pm, 66 (72, 78, 84) sts around armhole, pm, 6 (7, 8, 9) sts along dec area of armhole, 8 (9, 10, 11) sts along underarm. (94, 104, 114, 124 sts)

Knit 3 rows.

Change to larger needle.

Sl 14 (16, 18, 20) sts to RH needle.

Next row (RS): Join MC, beg with with first st after 2nd marker, k to next marker, remove marker, k1, turn, p back to next marker, remove it, p1.

Work short rows in this manner, extending each row 1 st beyond st of previous row until remaining markers are reached.

Next row (RS): *K to 1 st before next CC st, k2tog (1 MC st of sleeve and 1 CC st of underarm), turn, p to 1 st before next CC st, p2tog (1 MC st of sleeve and 1 CC st of underarm).

Rep from * until all underarm sts have been worked. (78, 86, 94, 102 sts)

Shape sleeve

[Dec 1 st each end every 6th row] 8 (6, 6, 6) times, then every 4th row 11 (15, 16, 17) times. (40, 44, 50, 56 sts)

Work even for 4 rows.

Change to smaller needle and CC.

Knit 4 rows, dec 9 (8, 9, 10) sts

evenly on last row. (31, 36, 41, 46 sts)

Cut yarn, leaving a 36-inch end. Leave sts on needle.

Cuff

With smaller needle and CC, cast on 10 sts.

Slipping first st of every row purlwise, work even in garter st in color sequence of 10 rows CC, then 10 rows MC until 60 (65, 70, 75) rows have been worked.

Bind off all sts.

Attach cuff to sleeve

Hold sleeve and cuff with RS tog, and with cuff in back of sleeve.

[Insert RH needle through sleeve st then into edge st of cuff, k2tog] twice, *bind off st on RH needle, insert RH needle through sleeve st then into next edge st of cuff, k2tog, rep from * until all sleeve and cuff sts have been joined.

Sew sleeve and side seam.

Neck Border

Beg at bottom of neck placket, with RS facing using smaller circular needle and CC, pick up and k 14 sts along side of placket, mark corner st, 9 (10, 11, 12) sts along neck front, 8 sts along curve of neck, 6 sts along side of neck, k 29 (31, 33, 35) sts of back neck, pick up and k 6 sts along side neck, 8 sts along curve of neck, 9 (10, 11, 12) sts along front neck, mark corner st, 14 sts down placket. (103, 107, 109, 111 sts)

Knit 3 rows, inc 1 st at each side of marked corner st on RS rows.

Mark for 3 buttonholes evenly spaced along right edge of placket.

Buttonhole row: [K to marker yo, k2tog] 3 times, work to end of row. Knit 2 rows, inc 1 st at each side of marked corner st on RS rows.

Bind off knitwise on WS.

Finishing

Sew ends of neck trim to bottom of placket, having right edge on top.

Sew on buttons. ❖

Panels in Plum Pullover

Design by Kennita Tully

You will be warm by the campfire in this paneled pullover.
The ringlet stitch is easy to do and the pattern knits up quickly.

Skill Level
Easy**

Size
Woman's small (medium, large)
Instructions are given for smallest size, with larger sizes in parentheses. When only 1 number is given, it applies to all sizes.

Finished Measurements
Chest: 36 (40, 44) inches
Length: 23 inches

Materials
- Plymouth Galway Highland Heather worsted weight 100 percent wool yarn (210 yds/100g per ball) 5 (6, 7) skeins medium plum heather #719
- Size 7 (4.5mm) 16- and 29-inch circular and straight needles
- Size 8 (5mm) needles or size needed to obtain gauge
- Stitch markers
- Tapestry needle

Gauge
17 st and 24 rows = 4 inches/10cm in pat st with larger needles
To save time, take time to check gauge.

Special Abbreviation
MR (Make Ringlet—worked over 2 sts): P2, wyif sl these 2 sts back to LH needle, going in front of the 2 sts take yarn around to back, sl the sts back to RH needle.

Pattern Notes
Sweater is worked by first knitting front and back center panels, then picking up sts along the side of both panels and knitting to the cuff.

Use long-tail method for all cast-on edges.

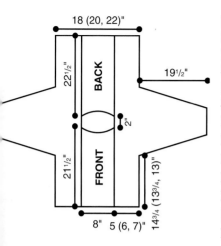

18 (20, 22)"

22½"

BACK

19½"

2"
2"

FRONT

21½"

14¾ (13¾, 13)"

8"   5 (6, 7)"

Back Panel

Cast on 36 sts.

Row 1: Purl.

Row 2: K15, [MR] 3 times, k15.

Rep Rows 1 and 2 until panel measures 22 inches.

Neck shaping

K4, join 2nd ball of yarn and bind off center 28 sts, k4.

Working on both sides of neck with separate balls of yarn, [dec 1 st at each neck edge] twice, bind off remaining 2 sts.

Front Panel

Cast on 36 sts.

Row 1 and all odd-numbered rows (WS): Purl.

Row 2: Knit.

Row 4: K7, MR, k6, [MR] 3 times, k6, MR, k7.

Row 6: K6, [MR] twice, k5, [MR] 3 times, k5, [MR] twice, k6.

Row 8: K5, [MR] 3 times, k4, [MR] 3 times, k4, [MR] 3 times, k5.

Row 10: K4, [MR] 4 times,

k3, [MR] 3 times, k3, [MR] 4 times, k4.

Row 12: K3, [MR] 5 times, k2, [MR] 3 times, k2, [MR] 5 times, k3.

Row 14: K2, [MR] 6 times, k1, [MR] 3 times, k1, [MR] 6 times, k2.

Row 16: Rep row 12.

Row 18: Rep row 10.

Row 20: Rep row 8.

Row 22: Rep row 6.

Row 24: Rep row 4.

[Rep Rows 1–24] 5 times, rep Row 1.

Beg neck shaping

K 9 sts, join 2nd ball of yarn and bind off center 18 sts, work across remaining 9 sts. Working on both sides of neck with separate balls of yarn, [bind off 2 sts at each neck edge] twice, then [dec 1 st every other row] 3 times. (2 sts)

Bind off.

Front panel should measure approximately 21½ inches.

Left Side

With RS facing, pick up and k 92 sts along right side of front panel, cast on 6 sts for neck, pick up and k 98 sts along left side of back panel. (196 sts)

Purl 1 row.

Ringlet Row: K1, MR across row to last st, k1.

Rep last 2 rows once more.

Set up pat: P85, pm, p26, pm, p to end of row. Markers denote center panel.

All WS rows: Purl.

Row 3: K1, *[MR] twice, k8, rep from * to marker, [MR] 3 times, k 14, [MR] 3 times, *k8, [MR] twice, rep from *, end with k1.

Row 5: K2, *[MR] twice, k8, rep from * to marker, end k7; [MR] 3 times, k6, MR, k6, [MR] 3 times, k7, [MR] twice, *k8, [MR] twice, rep from *, end k2.

Row 7: K3, *[MR] twice, k8; rep from * to marker, end k6; [MR] 3

times, k5, [MR] twice, k 5, [MR] 3 times, k6, [MR] twice, *k8, [MR] twice; rep from *, end k3.

Continue in this manner to work 1 diamond motif as before in center panel, and *at the same time* move ringlet st diagonally inward by 1 st each row until side section measures 5 (6, 7) inches, ending with a WS row.

Sleeves

Continuing in established pat, bind off 63 (59, 56) sts at beg of next 2 rows. Working on center 70 (78, 84) sts only, keeping to pat, beg sleeve shaping.

Shape sleeves

Dec 1 st at each end of next row, then [every 6th row] 19 more times. (30, 38, 44 sts)

When last diamond motif has been completed (6 in all), change to smaller needles.

Cuff

[Work 1 row of ringlet sts. Purl 1 row] 3 times.

Bind off all sts.

Right Side

Work as for left side, reversing shaping.

Neck Band

With 16-inch circular needles, pick up and k 36 sts along back neck, 6 sts along cast on edge, 38 sts along front neck and 6 sts along cast on edge. (86 sts)

[Work 1 rnd of ringlet st. Knit 1 rnd] 3 times.

Bind off.

Sew side seams.

Lower Band

With smaller circular needles, pick up and k along bottom edge 76 (84, 92) sts each for front and back. (152, 168, 184 sts)

Work 6 rnds of ringlet pat as for neck band.

Side-to-Side Lace Sweater

Design by Nazanin S. Fard

This V-neck pullover is knit from side to side, eliminating the need for shoulder seams.
The lace pattern adds just the right touch of elegance.

Skill Level

Intermediate***

Size

Woman's small (medium, large)
Instructions are given for smallest size, with larger sizes in parentheses. When only 1 number is given, it applies to all sizes.

Finished Measurements

Chest: 40 (42, 44) inches
Total length: 22 (24, 24) inches
Sleeve length: 20 inches

Materials

- Plymouth Encore DK weight 75 percent acrylic/25 percent wool yarn (150 yds/50g per ball): 7 (8, 10) balls light peach #597
- Size 5 (3.75mm) 29-inch circular needle
- Size 6 (4.25mm) 29-inch circular needle or size needed to obtain gauge
- Stitch holders

Gauge

21 sts and 30 rows = 4 inches/ 10cm in Steeple Lace pat with larger needles

To save time, take time to check gauge.

Pattern Stitches

Cable Cast On

*Insert RH needle between the last 2 sts of LH needle, wrap yarn around RH needle as if to knit and pull yarn through to make a new st, place new st on LH needle.

Rep from * until desired amount of sts have been cast on.

Steeple Lace

(multiple of 12 sts + 1)

Row 1 (WS) and all odd-numbered rows: Purl.

Row 2: K1, *yo, ssk, k7, k2tog, yo, k1, rep from * across.

Row 4: K2, *yo, ssk, k5, k2tog, yo, k3, rep from * across, end last rep k2.

Row 6: K3, *yo, ssk, k3, k2tog, yo, k5, rep from * across, end last rep k3.

Row 8: K4, *yo, ssk, k1, k2tog, yo, k7, rep from * across, end last rep k4.

Row 10: K5, *yo, sl 1, k2tog, psso, yo, k9, rep from * across, end last rep k5.

Rows 12, 14, 16 and 18: K1, *yo, ssk, k1, k2tog, yo, k1, rep from * across.

Rows 20–28: Rep Rows 2–10.

Pattern Notes

This sweater is worked from side-to-side with a lace panel at the cuffs and repeated again on the shoulders from front to back.

There are no shoulder seams.

Circular needles are used to accommodate the large number of sts. Do not join, work back and forth in rows.

Sweater

Beg at right sleeve with smaller needles, cast on 53 (57, 61) sts.

Work even in k1, p1 ribbing for 15 rows.

Change to larger needle and inc 8 sts evenly on last WS row. (61, 65, 69 sts)

Knit 10 rows in St st; work 28 rows of Steeple Lace pat.

To center pat st at the correct place, there should be (1, 2, 4) sts at each end of row.

At the same time [inc 1 st each end every 10th row] 7 times, then [every 6th row] 8 times. (91, 95, 99 sts)

Work even until sleeve measures 20 inches, end with a WS row.

Note number of rows that were worked even.

Body

With RS facing, using cable cast on technique, cast on 51 (55, 59) sts for right front.

Knit one row, turn, cast on (51, 55, 59) sts for back. (193, 205, 217 sts)

Work even until body measures 2½ (3½, 4½) inches above cast-on front and back sts.

Work 28 rows of Steeple Lace pat.

Work in St st for 4 more rows.

Divide front & back

Next row (RS): K 100 (105, 112) sts, sl next 93 (100, 105) sts to holder for back.

Shape right front neck

Bind off 10 sts for front neck and work to end of row.

[Bind off 4 sts at neck edge every other row] 10 times (50, 55, 62 sts)

Shape left front neck

Work in reverse order of right front, by [casting on 4 sts at neck edge every other row] 10 times, then [casting on 10 sts] once. (100, 105, 112 sts)

Sl all sts to holder.

Back

Sl back sts onto needle and work even for 6 inches.

Join front & back

Sl front sts from holder to needle and work even in St st for 4 rows.

Work 28 rows of Steeple Lace pat.

Change to St st and work even for 2½ (3½, 4½) inches more, ending with a WS row.

Left Sleeve

Bind off 51 (55, 59) sts for front and back at beg of next 2 rows. (91, 95, 99 sts)

Change to St st and work even for same amount of rows as noted on right sleeve.

[Dec 1 st each end every 6th row] 8 times, then [every 10 rows] 7 times, working pat st at same point as right sleeve. (61, 65, 69 sts)

Change to smaller needles and dec 8 sts on next row. (53, 57, 61 sts)

Work even in k1, p1 ribbing for 15 rows.

Bind off loosely in rib pat.

Bottom Bands

With smaller needles, pick up and k 73 (79, 85) sts along lower edge of front. Work in k1, p1 ribbing for 20 rows.

Bind off loosely.

Rep for back.

Neck Band

Beg at center back neck with smaller needles and RS facing, pick up and k 12 sts along back neck, 51 sts along left neckline, 1 st at front point of V-neckline, 51 sts along right neckline, and 13 sts on remaining half of back neck. (128 sts)

Mark center front st.

Work in k1, p1 ribbing for 10 rounds, dec 2 sts at front point every row as follows: Work to 1 st before marker, sl next 2 sts onto RH needle as if to k2tog, k 1, pass 2 slipped sts over last st.

Bind off loosely in rib.

Finishing

Sew side and underarm seams. ❖

Rose Tweed Cardigan

Design by Joyce Englund

If you're not a fan of sewing, then you will love this sweater.
The sleeves and saddle shoulder are joined as you knit the body.

Skill Level
Intermediate***

Size
Woman's small (medium, large, extra-large) Instructions are given for smallest size, with larger sizes in parentheses. When only 1 number is given, it applies to all sizes.

Finished Measurement
Chest (buttoned): 38 (40, 42, 44) inches

Materials
- Plymouth Encore Colorspun worsted weight 75 percent acrylic/25 percent wool yarn (200 yds/100g per ball): 5 (5, 6, 6) balls gray/rose tweed #7990
- Size 6 (4.25mm) needles
- Size 9 (5.5mm) straight and 29-inch circular needles
- Cable needle
- Stitch markers
- Stitch holders
- 7 (8, 8, 9) ¾-inch buttons

Gauge
18 sts and 23 rows = 4 inches/10cm in St st with larger needles

To save time, take time to check gauge

Pattern Stitch

Cable Pattern (panel of 13 sts)
Rows 1, 3, 7 and 11 (RS): P2, k9, p2.

Row 2 and all WS rows: K2, p9, k2.

Row 5: P2, sl next 3 sts to cn and hold at back, k3, k3 from cn, k3, p2.

Row 9: P2, k3, sl 3 sts to cn and hold at front, k3, k3 from cn, p2.

Row 12: Rep row 2.

Rep Rows 1–2 for pat.

Pattern Notes

Cuffs of cardigan are worked long enough to be turned back. If shorter cuffs are desired, adjust pattern accordingly.

Sleeves are joined to body at the same time as fronts are worked as follows:

To Join Left Front

At the end of a RS row, join last st of body to first st of sleeve by slipping last st of body, picking up next sleeve st with RH needle, and working ssk.

At the beg of a WS row, join next st of sleeve to first st of body by placing next sleeve st on LH needle and working p2tog through the back loops.

To Join Right Front

At beg of a RS row, join next st of sleeve to first body st by placing next sleeve st on LH needle and working k2tog.

At end of WS row, join last body st to sleeve by slipping last body st purlwise, placing next sleeve st on LH needle, sl last body st to LH needle and p2tog.

Sleeves

With smaller needles, cast on 39 (41, 45, 49) sts.

Work even in k1, p1 ribbing for 3½ (3¾, 4, 4) inches, inc 2 sts at center of sleeve on last WS row. (41, 43, 47, 51 sts)

Change to larger needles.

Set up pat (RS): K14 (15, 17, 19), pm, work cable pat over next 13 sts, pm, k14 (15, 17, 19).

Keeping sts between markers in Cable pat and remaining sts in St st, [inc 1 st each end every 6th row] 13 (14, 16, 18) times. (67, 71, 79, 87 sts)

Work even until sleeve measures 15 (16, 17, 18) inches above ribbing, ending with a WS row.

Place 25 (27, 31, 35) sts on either side of center cable on separate holders.

Continue to work in established pat on 17 center saddle sts only for an additional 5 (5, 5½, 6) inches.

Place saddle sts on separate holder.

Left Front

Pick up and k 25 (26, 28, 30) sts across 1 side of saddle for left front.

Working joining as explained in notes, join body to sleeve for 2 rows, then work 1 row of body even without joining.

Rep last 3 rows until all sleeve sts have been joined, *at the same time* inc 1 st at neck edge on 6th (8th, 8th, 10th) row, then every following RS row 4 more times. (30, 31, 33, 35 sts)

Work 1 WS row.

Next row (RS): Cast on 8 (10, 10, 12) sts for front neck. (38, 41, 43, 47 sts)

Continue in St st until sleeve is completely joined.

Place front sts on holder.

Right Front

Work right front as for left, reversing shaping.

Back

Pick up and k 28 (29, 33, 34) sts across back of left sleeve saddle, cast on 31 (33, 35, 37) sts for back of neck, pick up and k 28 (29, 33, 34) sts across back of right sleeve saddle. (87, 91, 101, 105 sts)

Continue to join at both sleeve edges as for fronts (2 rows joined, 1 row unjoined), until all sts of both sleeves have been worked.

Cut yarn.

Lower Body

Join yarn at left front edge.

K 38 (41, 43, 47) sts of left front, 87 (91, 101, 105) back sts, and 38 (41, 43, 47) sts of right front. (163, 173, 187, 199 sts)

Work even in St st until back measures 11 (12, 12½, 13) inches or 2 (2, 2½, 2½) inches less than desired length, ending with a WS row.

Change to smaller needles.

Ribbing

Row 1 (RS): K2, *p1, k1, rep from * to last 2 sts, k2.

Row 2: P2, *k1, p1, rep from * to last 2 sts, p2.

Rep Rows 1 and 2 until ribbing measures 2 (2, 2½, 2½) inches, ending with a WS row.

Bind off in pat, do not cut yarn.

Right Front Band

Pick up and k 85 (87, 89, 91) sts up front.

Making sure lower edge st is knitted, work in k1, p1 ribbing for 12 rows, making 6 (7, 7, 8) buttonholes evenly spaced. Last buttonhole will be placed in neck band.

Buttonholes: After k st, yo, k2tog on RS.

Bind off in ribbing.

Left Front Band

Beg at top of left front, work as for right front band, omitting buttonholes.

Neck Band

With RS facing, pick up and k 93 (95, 99, 101) sts around neck, dec evenly at saddles and as needed across back.

Work k1, p1 ribbing for 10 rows, making last buttonhole on row 6.

Bind off on RS.

Finishing

Sew sleeve seams.

Sew on buttons. ❖

A Touch of Norway

Design by Ann E. Smith

Using a steek and cutting your work, knit this multicolored cardigan with bands of traditional motifs for an introduction to Nordic knitting.

Skill Level
Intermediate***

Size
Woman's small (medium, large, extra-large) Instructions are given for smallest size, with larger sizes in parentheses. When only 1 number is given, it applies to all sizes.

Finished Measurements
Chest: 42 (44, 46, 48) inches
Length: 23 (24, 25, 26) inches

Materials
- Plymouth Encore Chunky bulky weight 75 percent acrylic/25 percent wool yarn (143 yds/100g per ball): 4 (4, 5, 6) balls charcoal #389 (MC), 3 skeins red #9601 (A), 1 skein each blue #133 (B), and soft white #146 (C)
- Size 7 (4.5mm) double pointed, 16- and 29-inch circular knitting needles
- Size 10 (6mm) 16- and 29-inch circular knitting needles or size needed to obtain gauge
- Stitch markers
- Yarn needle
- 3 decorative clasps

Gauge
15 sts and 19 rows = 4 inches/10cm in St st with larger needles
To save time, take time to check gauge.

Special Abbreviation
M1 (Make 1): Inc by making a backward loop over RH needle.

Sl m: Slip marker

Pattern Notes
The cardigan is worked in rnds of St st from neck to lower edge, all in 1 piece. The front is cut open

along steek sts so borders can be added.

Steek sts are not included in st counts; they are worked in St st, alternating MC and CC on patterned rnds.

When working with 2 colors in 1 row, carry unused strand loosely along WS of fabric.

Cardigan
Beg at neck with smaller 16-inch circular needle and MC, cast on 77 sts, pm, cast on 5 steek sts, pm.

Join without twisting.

Ribbing rnd: K1, *p1, k1, rep from * around.

Work even for 5 more rnds.

Change to larger needle.

Beg raglan shaping
Note: Two markers are in place to denote steek, 8 more will be added to

denote raglan seam lines.

Rnd 1: K12, M1, pm, k1, pm, M1, k10, M1, pm, k1, pm, M1, k29, M1, pm, k1, pm, M1, k10, M1, pm, k1, pm, M1, k12. (85 sts)

Rnd 2: Knit.

Rnd 3: [K to raglan marker, M1, sl m, k1, sl m, M1] 4 times, k to end of rnd. (93 sts)

Rnd 4: Knit.

Continue to [inc 8 sts every other rnd] 24 (26, 28, 30) times more, ending with a plain rnd. (285, 301, 317, 333 sts)

Divide for sleeves
Removing raglan markers, k38 (40,

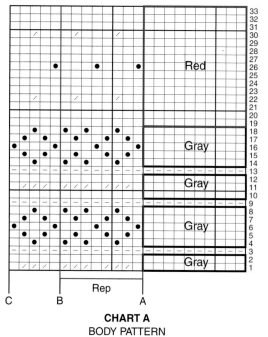

MOTIF PATTERN COLOR KEY
- ⊟ Red
- ⊠ Blue
- ⊙ White
- ☐ Background Color

MOTIF PATTERN   BACKGROUND COLOR

CHART A
BODY PATTERN

Dec Rnd: K1, ssk, k to last 3 sts, k2tog, k1.

Rnds 2–4: Knit 3 rnds.

[Rep last 4 rnds] 9 times. (46, 50, 54, 58 sts)

Join A and knit 3 rnds.

Rnd 4: With A, k1, ssk, k1, *k1 B, k3 A, rep from * to last 3 sts, k2tog, k1.

With A, knit 3 rnds.

Row 8: With A, k1, ssk, k2, *k1 C, k3 A, rep from * to last 3 sts, k2tog, k1.

With A, knit 3 rnds.

Row 12: With A, k1, ssk, k3, *k1 B, k3 A, rep from * to last 3 sts, k2tog, k1.

With A, knit 3 rnds.

Beg cuff

Change to smaller dpn.

Knit 1 rnd, dec 10 (14, 16, 18) sts evenly. (30, 30, 32, 34 sts)

Work even in k1, p1 ribbing until cuff measures 6 inches.

Bind off in pat.

Finishing

Cut a long strand of color C and

42, 44) for right front, k 64 (68, 72, 76) sts and place on a holder for right sleeve, k 81 (85, 89, 93) sts for back, k 64 (68, 72, 76) sts and place on 2nd holder for left sleeve, k 38 (40, 42, 44) sts for left front. (157, 165, 173, 181 sts)

Knit 1 rnd.

Lower Body

Referring to chart, work in color pat rep from A–B across, ending last rep at C.

Work rnds 1–25 once, [rep rnds 22–33] 3 times.

Change to smaller needle.

Work Ribbing rnd as for neck band for a total of 10 rnds.

Bind off in pat.

Sleeves

With RS facing using larger 16-inch circular needle and MC, k sts from holder, pm between first and last st. (64, 68, 72, 76 sts)

twice, knit 1 row for turning ridge, [knit 1 row, purl 1 row] 3 times.

Bind off loosely knitwise.

Turn facing to inside along turning ridge.

Sew facing in place so it covers zigzagged edge.

Right Front Band

Work as for left band, matching colors to those of cardigan body.

Sew clasps to front bands, having top one 1½ inch below top edge, and remainder each spaced 3½ inches below. ❖

thread into yarn needle. Make a basting line along center of middle st of steek.

With sewing machine, zigzag in st next to center basted st along length of entire front. Rep for opposite side.

Remove basting thread and cut center of middle st. You will be cutting through the horizontal bars only.

Turn back resulting facing on each side so first knit rib at top and bottom is at the edge.

Left Front Band

With RS facing using smaller needle and MC, pick up and k 60 sts evenly along turning row of gray area, with A pick up and k 33 sts evenly in red area to lower edge.

Working in appropriate colors to match front, [purl 1 row, knit 1 row]

Life in the City

Crescent Band Cardigan

Design by Kennita Tully

*An uncommon stitch pattern tipped on its side makes
a trendy cardigan that will stand out in the city crowd.*

Skill Level
Intermediate***

Size
Woman's small (medium, large, extra-large) Instructions are given for smallest size, with larger sizes in parentheses. When only 1 number is given, it applies to all sizes.

Finished Measurements
Chest: 36 (40, 44, 48) inches
Length: 19 (19½, 20, 21) inches

Materials
- Plymouth Indiecita worsted weight 100 percent Peruvian alpaca yarn (102 yds/50g per ball): 12 (13, 14, 16) balls pearl gray #401
- Size 6 (4.25mm) 29-inch circular needle
- Size 7 (4.5mm) 29-inch circular needle or size needed to obtain gauge
- Stitch markers
- Stitch holders
- Tapestry needle
- 3 (¾-inch) buttons

Gauge
23 sts and 34 rows = 4 inches/10cm in Banded Crescent pat

To save time, take time to check gauge.

Pattern Stitch

Crescent Band (multiple of 3 sts)
Row 1 (WS): Knit.

Rows 2 and 3: Purl.

Row 4: K3, *sl 1 wyib, k2, rep from * across row.

Row 5: P2, *sl 1 wyif, p2, rep from * across, end last rep sl 1 wyif, p3.

Row 6: K1, sl 2 wyib, drop next st off needle to front of work, replace first sl 2 sts back to LH needle, pick up dropped st and k it, k2, rep from * across, end last rep k2.

Row 7: Purl.

Row 8: K1, *k1, ssk, yo, rep from * across, end last rep k2.

Row 9: Purl.

Row 10: K1, *sl 1 wyib, k2, rep from * across, end last rep k2.

Row 11: P4, *sl 1 wyif, p2, rep from * across, end last rep sl 1 wyif, p1.

Row 12: K1, *drop next st off needle to front of work, k2, pick up dropped st and k it, rep from * across, end last rep k2.

Rep Rows 1–12 for pat.

Pattern Notes
Sweater is knit from right cuff to left cuff.

Circular needles are used to accommodate large number of sts. Work back and forth in rows, do not join.

Row gauge must be accurate for this pattern.

Make sure to keep careful track of rows.

Right Sleeve
Using long-tail method, cast on 39 (45, 51, 57) sts.

Beg with Row 1 of Crescent Band pat, [inc 1 st each side every 6th row] 14 times, then [every 8th row] 10 times. (87, 93, 99, 105 sts)

Work even until sleeve measures approximately 19¾ inches, ending with Row 11 of pat.

Body
Cast on 63 (63, 63, 66) sts onto RH

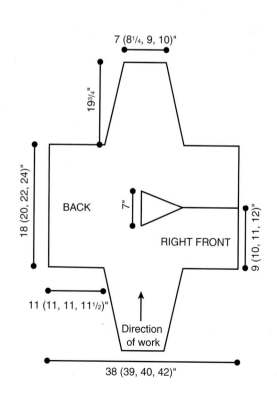

needle for right front, work across 44 (47, 50, 53) sts of sleeve, pm for shoulder seam, work across remaining 43 (46, 49, 52) sleeve sts, cast on 63 (63, 63, 66) sts for back. (213, 219, 225, 237 sts)

Work even in pat until body measures 5½ (6½, 7½, 8½) inches above cast-on sts, ending with a WS row.

Beg right front neck shaping

Next row (RS): Work to 2 sts before marker, k2tog, join 2nd ball of yarn, work to end of row. Mark this row at each end of back.

Working on both front and back with separate balls of yarn work even on back, *at the same time* [dec 1 st every row at front neck edge] 29 times more. (77, 80, 83, 89 sts)

Bind off front sts.

Beg back neck shaping

Working even in established pat on back sts only until back measures approximately 7 inches above marked row, ending with Row 7 of pat.

Place back sts onto holder.

Left Front

Cast on 77 (80, 83, 89) sts.

Work Row 1 of Crescent Band pat.

Working in established pat, [inc 1 st at neck edge every row] 30 times. Inc is made by knitting into front, then back of same st. (107, 110, 113, 119 sts)

Next row (RS): Beg with Row 8 of pat, work across front sts, sl back sts from holder to LH needle, work to end of row. (213, 219, 225, 237 sts)

Mark this row.

Work even until left side of body measures approximately 5½ (6½, 7½, 8½) inches above marker, ending with Row 3 of pat.

Left Sleeve

Bind off 63 (63, 63, 66) sts at beg of next 2 rows. (87, 93, 99, 105 sts)

Beg sleeve shaping

[Dec 1 st each end every 8th row] 10 times, then [every 6th row] 14 times. (39, 45, 51, 57 sts)

End with Row 3 of pat.

Bind off.

Sew sleeve and side seams.

Front Bands

With RS facing, beg 4 sts up from lower right front edge (to allow fabric to curl in) and working in each st, pick up and k 50 (53, 55, 61) sts along right front, [skipping next 3 sts of front cable cast-on 3 sts for buttonhole, pick up and k 7 sts] twice, cable cast-on 3 sts as before, pick up and k 35 sts along shaped edge of neck, 41 sts along back neck, 35 sts along left neckline and 73 (76, 78, 84) sts down left front. (257, 263, 267, 279 sts)

Purl 1 row, knit 1 row.

Bind off knitwise on WS.

Sew on buttons. ❖

City Sidewalks

Design by Lynnette Harter

*Texture and simple shaping combine to make a flattering
cardigan which is knit sideways from cuff to cuff.*

Skill Level
Intermediate***

Size
Woman's small (medium, large, extra-large) Instructions are given for smallest size, with larger sizes in parentheses. When only 1 number is given, it applies to all sizes.

Finished Measurements
Chest: 39 (42, 45, 48) inches
Length: 19½ (20, 20½, 21) inches

Materials
• Plymouth Galway Highland Heather worsted weight 100 percent wool yarn (210 yds/100g per ball): 6 (6, 7, 8) balls light plum heather #718
• Size 7 (4.5mm) 24-inch circular needle or size needed to obtain gauge
• Stitch markers
• Stitch holder
• Tapestry needle
• Size 7 (4.5mm) crochet hook
• 1 (1-inch) button

Gauge
18 sts and 28 rows = 4 inches/10cm in pat st

To save time, take time to check gauge.

Special Abbreviations
RT (right twist): K into 2nd st on LH needle, then k into first st, sl both sts off needle.

Inc: Increase by knitting (or purling) into the horizontal strand between needles.

Pattern Notes
Cardigan is worked in one piece from right sleeve to left sleeve.

Circular needle is used to accommodate large number of sts. Work in rows; do not join.

To make it easier to follow pat, place markers on each side of RT when working sleeves.

Keep very careful track of row counts to ensure sides are identical.

Right Sleeve

Cast on 46 (48, 50, 52) sts.

Rows 1–3: Knit.

Set up pat: Beg as indicated for chosen size, work Row 1 of Chart A over 22 (23, 24, 25) sts, pm, RT, pm, work Row 1 of Chart B over 22 (23, 24, 25) sts.

Working incs into pat, [inc 1 st each side of RT every 5th row] 20 (21, 21, 20) times. (86, 90, 92, 92 sts)

Work even in pat until sleeve measures 16¾ (17, 16¾, 16½) inches from beg, ending with a RS row.

Record number of rows worked after last inc row as X.

Right Front

Next row (WS): Work across 42 (44, 45, 45) sts and place on holder, inc 1 st for shoulder selvage

st, work in established pat across remaining sts, cast on 45 (45, 47, 49) sts at end of row. (90, 92, 95, 97 sts)

Row 2 (RS): K3, work in established chart A pat to last 3 sts, RT, k1.

Keeping 3 sts at front bottom edge in garter st, and 1 st at shoulder edge in St st, work in established pats until front measures 6½ (7, 7¾, 8½) inches above side cast-on edge, ending with a RS row.

Record number of rows worked on right front after cast-on edge as Y.

Shape neck edge

Row 1 (WS): K21, work to end in established pat.

Row 2: Work in pat to last 21 sts, k to end.

Row 3: Bind off 18, k3, work in pat to end. (72, 74, 77, 79 sts)

Keeping first and last 3 sts in garter st, work even in pat until front measures 9½ (10¼, 11, 11¾) inches above side cast-on edge, ending with a RS row.

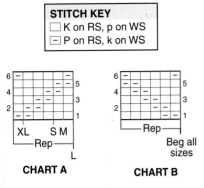

STITCH KEY
- ☐ K on RS, p on WS
- ⊟ P on RS, k on WS

CHART A

CHART B

Record number of rows worked from beg of right side neck edge as Z. Also record row number of last row worked.

Right Front Band

Buttonhole row (WS): K4, bind off 2, k to end.

Row 2: K to last 4 sts, cast on 2, k4.

Row 3: Knit.

Bind off all sts. Cut yarn.

Back—Right Half

Sl sleeve sts from holder to LH needle.

With RS facing, join yarn and cast on 1 st at shoulder edge for selvage st.

Row 1 (RS) K1, work in established pat to end of row, cast on 45 (45, 47, 49) sts. (88, 90, 93, 95 sts)

Row 2: K3, work in pat to last st, p1.

Keeping 1 st at shoulder edge in St st and 3 sts at back bottom edge in garter st, work even in established pats until back has same number of rows as recorded for Y, ending with a WS row.

Shape back neck

Row 1 (RS): K3, work in pat to end.

Keeping first and last 3 sts in garter st, work even in established pats until number of rows equal that as recorded for Z, ending with a WS row. Back should measure 9½ (10¼, 11, 11¾) inches above side cast-on edge.

Purl 3 rows for center back ridge.

Back—Left Half

Work as for right half of back, reversing shaping and substituting Chart B for Chart A, ending with a WS row.

You should have the same amount of rows for back neck as recorded for Z, and same number as recorded for Y for shoulder area.

Back should measure 9½ (10¼, 11, 11¾) inches from center back ridge.

Next row (RS): Work 43 (45, 46, 46) sts in pat and place on holder for half of left sleeve.

Bind off rem 45 (45, 47, 49) sts. Cut yarn.

Left Front

Cast on 72 (74, 77, 79) sts.

Rows 1–3: Knit.

Next row (RS): K3, beg with same

row as recorded for last row of right front, work chart B over next 66 (68, 71, 73) sts, k3.

Keeping first and last 3 sts in garter st and remaining sts in established pat, work even until front measures Z minus 3 rows, ending with a RS row.

Begin neck shaping

Cast on 18 sts at end of last RS row. (90, 92, 95, 97 sts)

Rows 1 and 3 (WS): K21, work in pat to last 3 sts, k1.

Row 2: K3, work in pat to last 21 sts, k21.

Row 4: K3, work in pat to last 3 sts, pm, RT, k1.

Keeping 1 st at shoulder edge in St st and 3 front bottom edge sts in garter st, work even in established pats until front measures Y minus 1 row.

Join side seams

Sl sts from holder to needle having shoulder edges tog.

Next row (RS): Bind off 45 (45, 47, 49) sts, work 44 (46, 47, 47) sts in pat, knit next st (shoulder selvage st) tog with left back selvage st, work in pat to end of row. (87, 91, 93, 93 sts)

Left Sleeve

Row 1 (WS): Work 41 (43, 44, 44) sts, work next 2 sts tog in pat, pm, work to end of row in pat. (86, 90, 92, 92 sts)

Work even in established pat for same number of rows as recorded for X.

Begin sleeve shaping

[Dec 1 st each side of RT every 5th row] 20 (21, 21, 20) times. (46, 48, 50, 52 sts)

Work even in pat for 4 or 5 more rows, in order to end with a RS row.

Knit 3 rows.

Bind off all sts.

Finishing

Sew shoulder and sleeve seams.

Sew side seams starting at underarm and continuing for 5 (5, 5¼, 5¼) inches.

Crochet a single ch on inside of back neck edge to stabilize neckline.

Sew button on left front opposite buttonhole. ❖

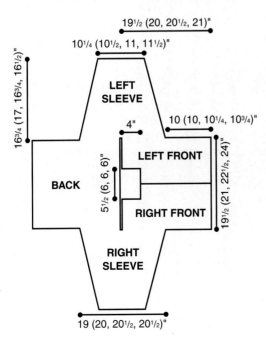

Lace Scallops Vest

Design by E. J. Slayton

Flowing scallops make this vest unique. It is worked from the shoulders downward to the scalloped bottom edge.

Skill Level
Advanced****

Size
Woman's small (medium, large, extra-large) Instructions are given for smallest size, with larger sizes in parentheses. When only 1 number is given, it applies to all sizes.

Finished Measurements
Chest: 34 (38, 42, 46) inches
Length: 22 (22, 24, 24) inches

Materials
- Plymouth Indiecita Baby Alpaca DK weight 100 percent Peruvian alpaca yarn (125 yds/50g per ball): 6 (6, 8, 9) balls dark green #1440
- Size 3 (3.25mm) needles or size needed to obtain gauge
- Stitch markers
- Tapestry needle
- 3 (⅝-inch) buttons

Gauge
23 sts and 31 rows = 4 inches/10cm in Lace Scallop pat
To save time, take time to check gauge.

Special Abbreviations
CDD (centered double decrease): Sl next 2 sts as if to k2tog, k1, p2sso.
M1 (make 1): Inc by making a backward loop over right needle.

Pattern Stitches

A. Lace Scallops (multiple of 12 sts + 1)
Rows 1 and 3 (RS): Purl.
Row 2 and all WS rows: Purl.
Row 5: Ssk, *k4, yo, k1, yo, k4, CDD, rep from *, end last rep k2tog instead of CDD.
Row 7: Ssk, *k3, yo, k2tog, yo, k1,

yo, k3, CDD, rep from *, end last rep k2tog instead of CDD.

Row 9: Ssk, *k2, yo, k2tog, yo, k1, yo, ssk, yo, k2, CDD, rep from *, end last rep k2tog instead of CDD.

Row 11: Ssk, *k1, yo, [k2tog, yo] twice, k1, yo, ssk, yo, k1, CDD, rep from *, end last rep k2tog instead of CDD.

Row 13: Ssk, *yo, [k2tog, yo] twice, k1, yo, [ssk, yo] twice, CDD, rep from *, end last rep k2tog instead of CDD.

Row 14: Purl.

Rep Rows 1–14 for pat.

B. Border

Row 1 (RS): *P1, p2tog, p3, M1, p1, M1, p3, p2tog, rep from * across, end p1.

Row 2: Purl.

Rows 3–7: Rep Rows 1 and 2, ending with Row 1.

Bind off knitwise on WS.

Pattern Notes

Keep 1 selvage st at each edge in St st throughout. These sts are not included in st counts, but are shown on charts.

Charts show beg and end for back shoulders, for body after underarm shaping, and fronts after shaping is completed.

When shaping armholes and neck, keep inc sts in St st until there are enough sts to work pat.

Work all inc and dec 1 st in from edge.

Buttonholes are made by binding off 3 sts on one row, then casting on 3 sts on the following row to complete buttonhole.

Back

Beg at shoulders, cast on 75 (87, 87, 99) sts. Mark center 43 (45, 45, 49) sts for back neck.

Referring to Chart A (B, B, A), work Row 1 of pat.

Work even in pat until back measures 6½ (6½, 7½, 8½) inches from beg, ending with a WS row.

Mark each end of this row.

Shape armholes

[Inc 1 st at each end every other row 6 times, then [cast on 6 sts at end of row] 2 (2, 4, 4) times. (99, 111, 123, 135 sts)

Work even in pat until back measures approximately 20 (20, 22, 22) inches from shoulder, ending with Row 14 of pat.

Border

Work Rows 1–7 of Border pat, making sure to line up inc and dec points with body pat.

STITCH KEY

- ☐ K on RS, p on WS
- ⊟ P on RS, k on WS
- ☐ Yo
- ☑ K2tog
- ☐ Ssk
- ☐ CDD
- ☒ M1
- ☑ P2tog

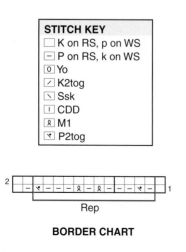

BORDER CHART

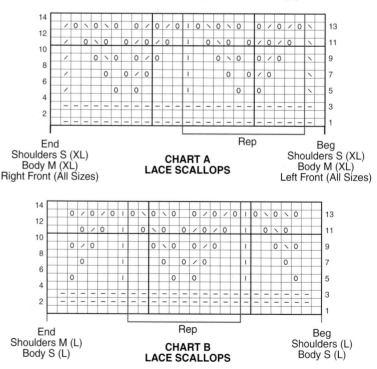

End
Shoulders S (XL)
Body M (XL)
Right Front (All Sizes)

**CHART A
LACE SCALLOPS**

Beg
Shoulders S (XL)
Body M (XL)
Left Front (All Sizes)

End
Shoulders M (L)
Body S (L)

**CHART B
LACE SCALLOPS**

Beg
Shoulders (L)
Body S (L)

Bind off knitwise on WS.

Fronts

With RS facing, pick up and k 16 (21, 21, 25) sts across right shoulder from armhole to first neck marker, attach 2nd ball of yarn, pick up and k 16 (21, 21, 25) sts across left shoulder from 2nd marker to end.

Next row: P1, k to last st, p1.

Beg with Row 3 of Chart A, work even in pat for 14 (14, 20, 24) rows from picked-up row.

Shape neck

Next RS row: [Inc 1 st at each neck edge every other row] 23 (24, 24, 26) times, *at the same time* when front measures same as back to beg of armhole shaping, shape armholes as for back.

Mark last row of neck shaping at each neck edge. (51, 57, 63, 69 sts each side)

Work even in established pat until fronts measure same as back.

Work border pat.

Bind off knitwise on WS.

Armbands

Beg at underarm with RS facing, pick up and k 1 st in each cast on st, pm, 3 sts for every 4 rows to beg of armhole shaping, 2 sts for every 3 rows to shoulder, pm, pick up and k same number of sts across other side of armhole.

Replace armhole corner markers with a safety pin in 7th (7th, 13th, 13th) st from each end.

Row 1 (WS): P1, k to last st, p1.

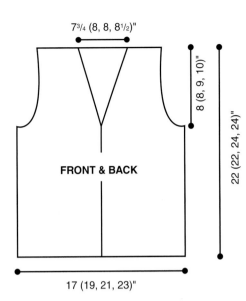

Row 2: [K to 1 st before marker, CDD] twice, k to end.

Rows 3–5: Rep Rows 1 and 2, ending with Row 1.

Bind off all sts purlwise on RS.

Front Band

Beg at bottom right front corner with RS facing, pick up and k 2 sts for every 3 rows to neck shaping, pm, 3 sts for every 4 rows along neck shaping, pm, 2 sts for every 3 rows to shoulder, pm, 1 st in each cast on st across neck back, pm, pick up and k same number of sts along left front.

Note: *Sl first st of every row purlwise wyif.*

Rows 1 and 3 (WS): Sl 1, k to end.

Rows 2 and 4: Sl 1, ssk, k to first marker, sl marker, M1, k to last marker, M1, sl marker, k to last 3 sts, k2tog, k1. Beg at neck shaping, mark right band for 3 buttonholes, having top one at neck shaping and remainder spaced 2½ inches apart.

Row 5 (WS): Sl 1, [k to marker, make buttonhole] 3 times, k to end.

Row 6: Rep Row 2, dec 4 sts evenly across back neck.

Rows 7 and 8: Rep Rows 1 and 2.

Bind off all sts knitwise on WS.

Finishing

Sew underarm seams.

Sew buttons on left band. ❖

Cable & Bobbles Vest

Design by Mary J. Saunders

The cable and bobble panel highlights an unusual vest.
Optional patch pockets give it versatility.

Skill Level
Intermediate***

Size
Woman's small (medium, large)
Instructions are given for smallest size, with larger sizes in parentheses. When only 1 number is given, it applies to all sizes.

Finished Measurements
Chest: 38 (42, 48) inches

Materials
- Plymouth Encore DK weight 75 percent acrylic/25 percent wool yarn (150 yds/50g per ball): 6 (8, 10) balls rose #180
- Size 5 (3.75mm) needles or size needed to obtain gauge
- Cable needle
- Size D/3 crochet hook
- Tapestry needle
- 1 (¾-inch) button

Gauge
20 sts and 40 rows (20 ridges) = 4 inches/10cm in garter st
To save time, take time to check gauge.

Special Abbreviations
M1 (make 1): Insert LH needle from back to front under bar between last st worked and next st, work this st by inserting RH needle into front loop, twisting st.

MB (make bobble): (K1, yo, k1, yo, k1) in same st. (5 sts)

Turn, p5, turn, k5, turn, p5, [pass 2nd st on LH needle over first st, then off needle] 3 times, k2tog.

RC (right cable): Sl 3 sts to cn and hold in back of work, k3, k3 from cn

LC (left cable): Sl 3 sts to cn and hold in front of work, k3, k3 from cn

RT (right twist): Sl 2 sts to cn and hold in back of work, k3, p2 from cn

LT (left twist): Sl 3 sts to cn and hold in front of work, p2, k3 from cn

Pattern Notes
This garter-st vest begins at mid-back, goes up over the shoulders, and down to the center front. After joining fronts and back, the vest takes a new direction with a horizontal cable band. It is finished with a garter-st bottom and optional patch pockets.

Yoke
Starting at mid-back, cast on 70 (72, 84) sts.

Knit 1 row and mark this as RS.

Slipping first st of each row, work even in garter st until yoke measures 1 (2, 3) inches, ending with a WS row.

Begin armhole shaping
Dec row: Sl 1, k1, k2tog, k to last 4 sts, k2tog, k2.

Knit 9 rows.

[Rep dec row every 10th row] 4 times more. (60, 62, 74 sts)

Begin neck shaping

Next row: Work across 25 (28, 32) sts, bind off center 10 sts, join 2nd ball of yarn and k remaining 25 (28, 32) sts.

Working on both sides of neck with separate balls of yarn, [dec 1 st at each neck edge every 10th row] 8 times. (17, 20, 24 sts each side of neck)

Work even until yoke measures 11 (12, 13) inches from beg, mark as top of shoulder. Work even for 2 inches more for front.

Begin V-neck shaping

Inc row: Sl 1, k1, M1, knit to last 2 sts, M1, k2.

Knit 9 rows.

[Rep inc row every 10th row] 17 times more. (35, 38, 42 sts)

Work even until yoke measures 22 (24, 26) inches from beg, ending with a WS row.

Body

Sl sts of right front to holder, cut yarn.

Knit across 35 (38, 42) sts of left front, cast on 22 (29, 34) sts for left underarm, working through both loops of cast-on edge pick up and k 70 (72, 84) sts along back, cast on 22 (28, 34) sts for right underarm, k across 35 (38, 42) sts of right front from holder. (184, 204, 236 sts)

Continue to sl first st of each row, knit 3 rows.

[Knit 1 row, purl 1 row] twice.

Next row: K1, *MB, k3, rep from * across, end last rep MB, k2.

Purl 1 row, knit 1 row, purl 2 rows.

Next row: P2 (6, 0), *p2, M1, rep from * across, end last rep p4 (8, 0). (273, 305, 353 sts)

Cast on 28 sts at end of last row.

Cable Panel

Row 1 (RS): P4, k3, p4, k6, p4, k3, p3, p2tog (last st of cable panel and one st from body), sl 1, turn.

Row 2 and all WS rows: K2tog, then k the knit sts and p the purl sts.

Row 3: P4, k3, p4, LC, p4, k3, P3, p2tog, sl 1, turn.

Rows 5: P4, k3, p4, k6, p4, k3, p3, p2tog, sl 1, turn.

Row 7: P4, LT, p2, k6, p2, RT, p3, p2tog, sl 1, turn.

Row 9: P6, LT, LC, RT, p5, p2tog, sl 1, turn.

Row 11: P8, [RC] twice, p7, p2tog, sl 1, turn.

Row 13: P6, RT, LC, LT, p5, p2tog, sl 1, turn.

Row 15: P4, RT, p2, k6, p2, LT, p3, p2tog, sl 1, turn.

Row 16: Rep Row 2.

Rep Rows 1–16 until 1 body st remains. Rep Row 1.

Bind off knitwise, leaving last loop on needle.

Lower Body

With WS facing, pick up and p 199 (227, 263) sts evenly along long side of cable panel.

Slipping first st of each row, purl 2 rows, knit 1 row.

Next row (RS): K3, *MB, k3, rep from * to end of row.

Purl 1 row, knit 1 row, purl 1 row.

Work even in garter st for 9 inches, or until desired length.

Bind off.

Pockets

(optional)

Make 2

Cast on 25 sts.

Work in garter st until pocket measures 4 inches.

Next row: *K2, M1, rep from * across, end last rep k1. (37 sts)

Cast on 10 sts at end of last row.

Cable Border

Rows 1 and 5 (RS): Sl 1, p1, k6, p1, sl 1 wyif, turn.

Rows 2, 4 and 6: K2tog, k1, p6, k2.

Row 3: Sl 1, p1, RC, p1, p2tog, sl 1 wyif, turn.

[Rep Rows 1–6] 6 times, then rep Row 1 once.

Bind off.

Finishing

Sew pockets in place, having side edge 2½ inches in from center front and bottom edges even.

Beg at center back, work 1 row sc around entire vest, making a 5-ch loop at top row of bobbles on right edge.

Beg at underarm, work 1 row sc around armhole.

Sew button at left front edge to match button loop. ❖

Night on the Town

Design by Joan McGowan-Michael

This luscious mohair sweater pairs perfectly with black slacks.
It is dressy enough to wear for a night of adventure in the city.

Skill Level

Intermediate***

Size

Woman's extra-small (small, medium, large) Instructions are given for smallest size, with larger sizes in parentheses. When only 1 number is given, it applies to all sizes.

Finished Measurements

Chest: 34 (36, 38, 40) inches

Hips: 36½ (38½, 40½, 42½) inches

Length from shoulder: 21¾ (21¾, 22½, 22½) inches

Sleeve length: 16½ (16½, 17½, 17½) inches

Sleeve at underarm: 14 (14½, 15, 16) inches

Materials

- Plymouth Le Fibre Nobili Collection—Lane Cervinia Imperiale mohair worsted weight 80 percent kid mohair/20 percent nylon yarn (109 yds/25g per ball): 9 (9, 10, 10) balls red #4111
- Size 8 (5mm) needles or size needed to obtain gauge
- Stitch markers
- Tapestry needle
- Straight pins

Gauge

14 sts and 24 rows = 4 inches/10cm in garter st

To save time, take time to check gauge.

Special Abbreviation

Wrap: Work the designated number of sts, sl next st to RH needle, bringing yarn from back to front between sl st and next st, moving sl st back to left hand needle (1 st wrapped), turn work and knit back in other direction to end. This counts as 2 rows.

Pattern Notes

Entire garment is worked in garter st from side seam to side seam. Because of this, make sure your row gauge is accurate.

Keep in mind that knitting worked sideways has a tendency to grow slightly in the wearing; the body and sleeves will lengthen by 1 to 1½ inches during wear.

The lace of the sleeves is not an edging but part of the entire sleeve. Short rows are used for the subtle shaping in the sleeves, body and collar.

Short rows are worked by wrapping sts.

Back

Beg at side seam, cast on 49 (49, 52, 52) sts. Mark last st as bottom edge.

Next row: K 21 sts, pm, k to end of row.

Knit 1 row.

Short row shaping

[K20, wrap next st, turn, k to end of row. K 2 rows] twice.

Work even on all sts for 8 (10, 12, 14) more rows.

Begin armhole

Next row: K to end of row, cast on 27 sts for left armhole. (76, 76, 79, 79 sts)

Knit 6 rows.

Begin neck shaping

[Dec 1 st at neck edge every other row] 4 times.

Knit 56 (58, 60, 62) rows.

[Inc 1 st at neck edge every other row] 4 times.

Knit 6 rows.

Bind off 27 sts at beg of next row for right armhole. (49, 49, 52, 52 sts)

Knit 8 (10, 12, 14) rows.

[K20, wrap next st, turn, k to end of row. K 2 rows] twice.

Knit 2 rows.

Bind off.

Front

Work as for back.

Sleeves

Cast on 49 (49, 53, 53) sts.

K36 (36, 40, 40), pm, work Row 1 of Chart A.

Continue with charts for chosen size as follows:

Size extra-small: [Work Chart A] 6 times.

Size small: Work Chart A once, [Chart B] 4 times, rep Chart A.

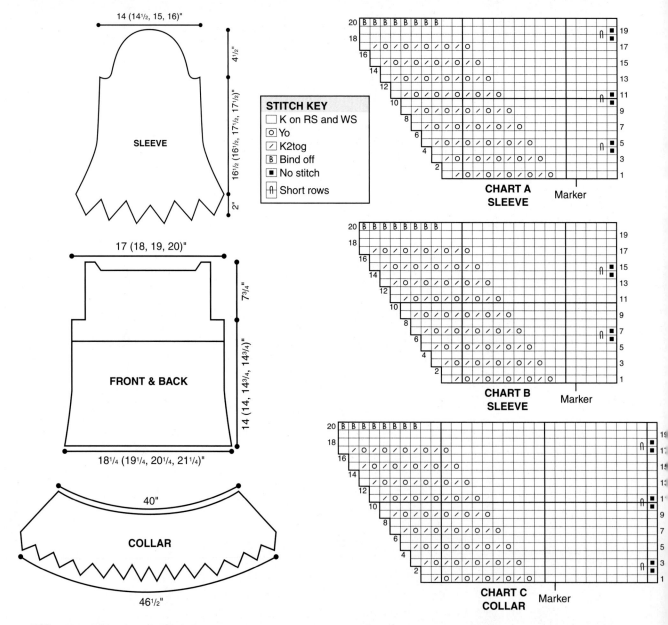

STITCH KEY
- ☐ K on RS and WS
- ◉ Yo
- ╱ K2tog
- Ⓑ Bind off
- ■ No stitch
- ⋒ Short rows

CHART A SLEEVE — Marker

CHART B SLEEVE — Marker

CHART C COLLAR — Marker

SLEEVE

14 (14½, 15, 16)"

4½"

16½ (16½, 17½, 17½)"

2"

FRONT & BACK

17 (18, 19, 20)"

7¾"

14 (14, 14¾, 14¾)"

18¼ (19¼, 20¼, 21¼)"

COLLAR

40"

46½"

Size medium: Work Chart B once, [Chart A] 4 times, rep Chart B.

Size large: [Work Chart B] 6 times.

At the same time at opposite end of sleeve, shape cap as follows:

Knit 9 (11, 13, 15) rows.

[Cast on 2 sts every other row] 9 times. (54, 54, 58, 58 sts between marker and end of sleeve cap)

Knit 30 rows.

[Bind off 2 sts every other row] 9 times.

Knit 9 (11, 13, 15) rows.

Bind off.

Collar

Cast on 24 sts.

Knit one row.

Referring to Chart C, [rep 20 rows] 14 times.

Bind off.

Sew bound-off edge to cast-on edge.

Finishing

Block all pieces lightly.

Sew shoulder seams.

Sew sleeves into armhole.

Sew sleeve and side seams.

Fold collar into fourths, having seam as one of the folds. Pm at each fold along straight edge of collar.

Pin right side of collar to wrong side of body, having st marker at center back, and remaining markers at each shoulder and center front.

Sew collar in place.

Flip collar to outside of sweater. ❖

Contrapposto Symphony Sweater

Design by Barbara Venishnick

Great paintings and sculptures inspired this angular sweater. The tasseled, slanted collar and dissimilar sleeves balance the asymmetrical lower edge.

Skill Level

Intermediate***

Size

Woman's small (medium, large) Instructions are given for smallest size, with larger sizes in parentheses. When only 1 number is given, it applies to all sizes.

Finished Measurements

Finished width: 22 (23½, 25) inches
Finished length: 20 inches on short side; 29 (29½, 30) inches on long side

Materials

- Plymouth Encore Chunky bulky weight 75 percent acrylic/25 percent wool yarn (143 yds/100g per skein): 8 (9, 9) skeins stone #240
- Size 10½ (6.5mm) 29-inch circular needle or size needed to obtain gauge
- 3½-inch piece cardboard
- Tapestry needle

Gauge

13 sts and 22 rows = 4 inches/10cm in Garter Stripe pat

To save time, take time to check gauge.

Pattern Stitches

Cable Cast-on: *Insert RH needle between first and 2nd st of LH needle, pull up a st and place it on LH needle creating a new first st. Rep from * for desired amount of sts.

Garter Stripe Pattern

Row 1 (RS): Knit.
Rows 2 and 3: Knit.
Row 4: Purl.
Rep Rows 1–4 for pat.

Pattern Notes

This sweater is knit in one piece from cuff to cuff. At the neck the work is divided in half for front and back, and both halves are worked at the same time. They are rejoined at the end of the neck opening.

The collar is worked from the narrow point to the wider end. Both halves are worked at the same time.

Row gauge must be accurate for this project. Keep careful track of rows.

Keep 1 st as a selvage at each end of every row as follows: at beg of every row k1-tbl; at end of every row sl 1 wyif.

All st counts include selvage sts.

Incs are made after first st and before last st by picking up the bar between sts with LH needle and knitting into the back of the st to twist it.

Dolman (Left) Sleeve

Beg at left sleeve, cast on 27 sts.

Work even in Garter Stripe pat for 4 rows.

[Inc 1 st each side every other row] 46 times. (119 sts)

Work even for 4 rows, ending with Row 2 of pat.

Front & Back

Working in established pat, cable cast on 8 sts at beg of next 2 rows. (135 sts)

Keeping first and last st as selvage st, [inc 1 st each side on every Row 1 of pat] 9 (10, 11) times. (153, 155, 157 sts)

When last inc is complete, work Row 2 once more.

Divide for neck

Beg with Row 3 of pat, work across first 76 (77, 78) sts, join 2nd ball of yarn and bind off 1 st, work across remaining 76 (77, 78) sts.

Establishing a selvage st on each side of neck opening, work even on neck edges, *at the same time* [continue inc at each bottom edge every 4th row as established] 12 times more. (88, 89, 90 sts on each side of neck opening)

Close neck & rejoin for shoulder

Beg with Row 1 of pat, work in established pat to neck edge, k selvage st, with same ball of yarn cable cast on 1 st, k this st and work to end of row, inc 1 st at end of row as established.

Cut 2nd ball of yarn.

Continue in pat, [working incs every 4th row as established] 9 (10, 11) times more. (197, 199, 201 sts)

Row 2 of pat has just been completed

Narrow (Right) Sleeve

Bind off 63 (64, 65) sts at beg of next 2 rows. (71 sts)

Reestablish selvage sts on each side of sleeve, work 4 rows even.

[Dec 1 st each side on every Row 1 of pat] 22 times. (27 sts)

Work even until right sleeve measures same as left, ending with a RS row.

Bind off all sts knitwise.

Collar

Cast on 3 sts, with 2nd ball of yarn cast on 3 more sts to same needle.

Rows 1 and 2: [k1-tbl, k1, sl 1] twice
Row 3: First half: k1-tbl, inc, k1, sl 1 2nd half: k1-tbl, k1, inc, sl 1.
Row 4: First half: k1-tbl, k2, sl 1; 2nd half: k1-tbl, k2, sl 1.

Continue in garter st, [inc 1 st on each side of collar at each outer edge every 4th row as established] 16 times more. (20 sts on each side of collar)

Note: Inside edge is worked even using a selvage st as established.

Work 1 WS row.

Join collar halves

With RS facing, k across all 40 sts with 1 ball of yarn.

Cut 2nd ball of yarn leaving a long tail for sewing.

Continue [working incs on each side every 4th row as established] 6 times. (52 sts)

Bind off loosely on WS knitwise.

Finishing

Pin collar to neck opening, having WS of collar to RS of sweater. Place long end of collar toward Dolman sleeve side of sweater and narrow points toward narrow sleeve. Narrow points of collar will extend past neck opening by approximately 1½ inches.

Sew center edges of collar to neck edge of sweater.

Sew 2 narrow points of collar tog.

Sew Dolman sleeve seam and short side seam.

Sew seam of narrow sleeve.

Sew long side seam, leaving approximately 9 (9, 10) inches above lower edge open.

Tassels
Make 2

Wrap yarn around a 3½-inch piece of cardboard about 22 times.

With a separate strand of yarn

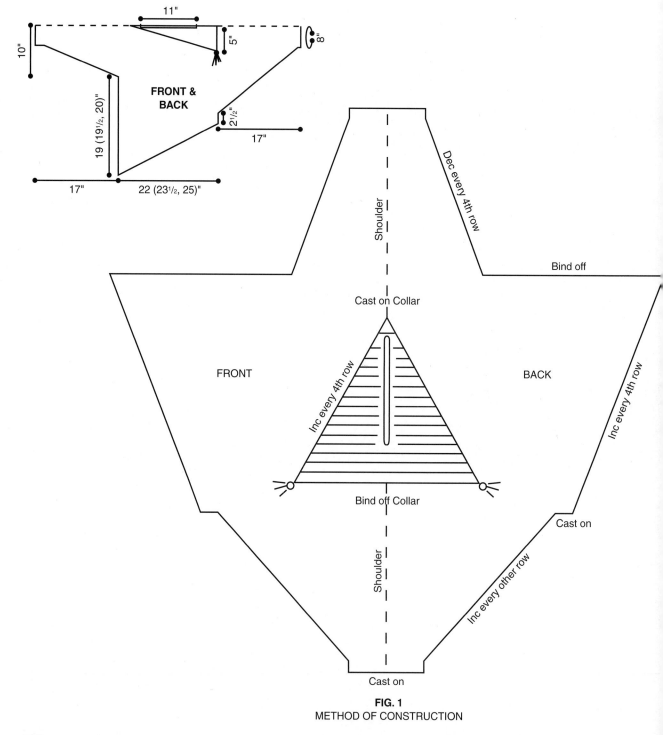

FIG. 1
METHOD OF CONSTRUCTION

...hreaded through a tapestry needle, wrap yarn through the center of the "hank" at 1 end. Tie very tightly and cut yarn leaving a long tail.

Cut tassel at opposite end. Hold tassel at the cut end and wrap another strand of yarn around the entire tassel about ¾ inch down from the tied end.

Tie 2nd strand very tightly.

Cut this strand of yarn and bury ends inside tassel.

Trim cut ends of tassel evenly.

Using long tails, sew tassel to 1 corner of the long end of collar.

Rep on other side of collar. ❖

City Evening Jacket

Design by Barbara Venishnick

You may never have seen cables positioned like this before! This jacket takes an Aran cable, along with three-by-three ribs, and twists them into an intriguing new silhouette.

Skill Level
Advanced****

Size
Woman's small (medium, large)
Instructions are given for smallest size, with larger sizes in parentheses. When only 1 number is given, it applies to all sizes.

Finished Measurements
Width at underarm: 22 (24, 25) inches

Length: back: 28 inches, front: 25 inches

Materials
- Plymouth Encore Chunky bulky weight 75 percent acrylic/25 percent wool yarn (143 yds/100g per skein): 10 (11, 12) skeins ivory #146
- Size 10 (6mm) straight and 29-inch circular needles or size needed to obtain gauge
- 2 (1-inch) buttons
- Cable needle
- Large crochet hook

Gauge
15 sts and 18 rows = 4 inches/10cm in Slanted Rib pat

To save time, take time to check gauge.

Special Abbreviations
C3F (cable 3 front): Sl 2 sts to cn and hold in front, p1, k2 from cn.

C3B (cable 3 back): Sl 1 st to cn and hold in back, k2, p1 from cn.

C4B (cable 4 back): Sl 2 sts to cn and hold in back, k2, k2 from cn.

C4F (cable 4 front): Sl 2 sts to cn and hold in front, k2, k2 from cn.

SS (selvage st): These are used at outer edges and at sleeve edges. At beg of every row, k1-tbl. At end of every row sl 1 wyif.

Pattern Stitches

Provisional Cast-on
With scrap yarn and a large crochet hook, loosely ch number of sts desired plus a few extra. With working yarn and needle, pick up 1 st in the back purl bump of each ch st until desired number of sts are on the working needle.

Cable Cast-on
*Insert RH needle between first and 2nd st on LH needle, wrap yarn and

pull up a lp. Place lp on LH needle creating a new first st. Rep from * until desired number of sts have been added.

A. Cable Panel

Row 1 (WS): K1, p1, k1, p2, k4, p2, k2, p2, k4, p2, k1, p1, k1.

Row 2: P1, sl 1, C3F, p3, k2, p2, k2, p3, C3B, p1, sl 1, p1.

Row 3: K1, p1, k2, p2, k3, p2, k2, p2, k3, p2, k2, p1, k1.

Row 4: P1, sl 1, p2, C3F, [p2, k2] twice, p2, C3B, p2, sl 1, p1.

Row 5: K1, p1, k3, [p2, k2] 3 times, p2, k3, p1, k1.

Row 6: P1, sl 1, p3, C3F, p1, k2, p2, k2, p1, C3B, p3, sl 1, p1.

Row 7: K1, p1, k4, p2, k1, p2, k2, p2, k1, p2, k4, p1, k1.

Row 8: P1, sl 1, p4, C3F, k2, p2, k2, C3B, p4, sl 1, p1.

Row 9: K1, p1, k5, p4, k2, p4, k5, p1, k1.

Row 10: P1, sl 1, p5, C4B, p2, C4F, p5, sl 1, p1.

Rows 11, 13, 15, 17 and 19: Rep Row 9.

Row 12: P1, sl 1, p5, k4, p2, k4, p5, sl 1, p1.

Rows 14 and 18: Rep Row 10.

Row 16: Rep Row 12.

Row 20: P1, sl 1, p4, C3B, k2, p2, k2, C3F, p4, sl 1, p1.

Row 21: Rep Row 7.

Row 22: P1, sl 1, p3, C3B, p1, k2, p2, k2, p1, C3F, p3, sl 1, p1.

Row 23: Rep Row 5.

Row 24: P1, sl 1, p2, C3B, [p2, k2] 2 times, p2, C3F, p2, sl 1, p1.

Row 25: Rep Row 3.

Row 26: P1, sl 1, p1, C3B, p3, k2, p2, k2, p3, C3F, p1, sl 1, p1.

Rep Rows 1–26 for pat.

B. Left Leaning Rib

Row 1 (WS): P3, k3.

Row 2: K1, p3, k2.

Row 3: P2, k3, p1.

Row 4: K2, p3, k1.

Row 5: P1, k3, p2.

Row 6: K3, p3.

Rep Rows 1—6 for pat.

C. Right Leaning Rib

Row 1 (WS): K3, p3.

Row 2: K2, p3, k1.

Row 3: P1, k3, p2.

Row 4: K1, p3, k2.

Row 5: P2, k3, p1.

Row 6: P3, k3.

Rep Rows 1–6 for pat.

Pattern Notes

The center back cable panel is worked first, then each side is worked from the sleeve cuff to the center, casting on sts for front and back. Each half is then sewn to the center back cable panel.

A selvage st is used at outer edges and sleeve edges. Selvage sts are included in st counts.

Circular needle is used to accommodate large number of sts. Work back and forth in rows.

Incs are made after first st and before last st by picking up the bar between sts with LH needle and knitting into the back of the st to twist it.

Center Back Panel

Note: Do not use selvages on this piece.

With straight needles, cast on 24 sts.

Work even in Cable Panel pat for 25 (25¼, 25½) inches.

Bind off loosely.

Left Half

Sleeves

With circular needle, cast on 50 sts.

Set up pat: SS, Row 1 of Left Leaning Rib pat over 12 sts, pm, Cable Panel pat over 24 sts, pm, Right Leaning Rib pat over 12 sts, SS.

Working in established pats, [inc 1 st each side every 4th row] 22 times. (94 sts)

Work even until sleeve measures 17 inches from beg, ending with a WS row.

Body

With RS facing, provisionally cast on 49 sts for back, work across 94 sts of sleeve, provisionally cast on 49 sts for front. (192 sts)

Reestablish selvage sts at beg and end of row, and incorporate new sts into rib patterns as established.

Shape lower edges

Making incs on RS rows, [inc 1 st at beg of every 4th row] 9 (10, 11) times for lower back edge, *at the same time* [inc 1 st at the end of every 8th row] 4 (5, 6) times for lower front edge. (205, 207, 208 sts)

Work even until body measures 7½ (8½, 9½) inches above provisional cast-on edge.

Divide for neck opening

Place last 88 (89, 90) sts of front and 24 sts of cable on holder.

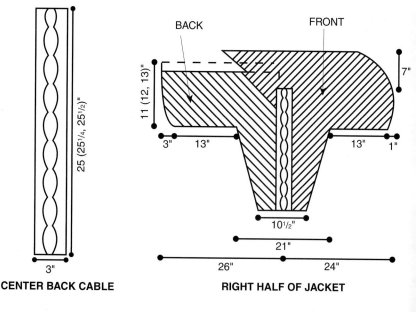

CENTER BACK CABLE

RIGHT HALF OF JACKET

Working on 93 (94, 95) sts of back only, continue to [inc 1 st every 4th row] twice more. (95, 96, 97 sts)

Work even for 4 more rows.

Bind off all back sts loosely.

Left Front

Sl front and cable sts from holder to needle.

With RS facing, cable cast on 13 sts for collar at beg of row.

Note: Cable Panel pat ends now.

Work across row, incorporating new sts and former cable sts into Right Leaning RIb pat as established.

With RS facing, [inc 1 st at beg of every 4th row] 9 times for collar, *at the same time* [dec 1 st at end of every 4th row] 9 times for lower front edge.

Bind off all sts loosely in pat.

Right Side

Work sleeve and provisional cast on as for left side.

Reversing shaping, work until body measures 7½ (8½, 9½) inches above provisional cast on.

Divide for neck opening

Work across first 88 (89, 90) sts of front and 24 sts of cable and place on holder, work remaining 93 [94, 95] sts for back.

Work right back as for left, reversing all shaping.

Right Front

Return front and cable sts to needle.

With WS facing, cable cast on 13 sts for collar at beg of row. Work across row, incorporating new sts and Cable Panel sts into rib pattern as established.

With RS facing, [dec 1 st at beg of every 4th row for bottom edge], and [inc 1 st at end of every 4th row for collar] 9 times, *at the same time* make buttonholes as follows:

First buttonhole (made on same row as 3rd dec/inc): Work across 27 (28, 29) sts, join 2nd ball of yarn and work to end of row, creating a slit for buttonhole. Continue to work with 2 balls of yarn for 3 more rows.

Next row (made on 4th dec/inc row): Work across with 1 ball of yarn

closing buttonhole. Cut 2nd ball of yarn, leaving a long tail.

Second buttonhole: Rep this process on 7th dec/inc row and close on 8th dec/inc row.

Work right front as for left.

Finishing

With long tail, work buttonhole st around each buttonhole.

Sew sleeve seams.

Side Seams

(See Fig. 1) Undo crochet ch and place front sts on 1 and back sts on 2nd.

Hold needles parallel with RS tog,

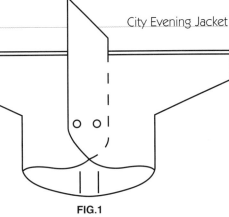

FIG.1
ASSEMBLED JACKET

and with 3rd needle work 3-needle bind off.

Sew center collar seam.

Sew bottom edge of collar to back neck edge.

Sew buttons under buttonholes. ❖

Downtown Excursion Jacket

Design by Diane Zangl

This jacket is an adaptation of the Moebius Vest by Elizabeth Zimmermann. With gracious permission from her daughter, Meg Swansen, we present a sleeved version.

Skill Level
Intermediate***

Size
Woman's small (medium, large, extra-large) Instructions are given for smallest size, with larger sizes in parentheses. When only 1 number is given, it applies to all sizes.

Finished Measurements
Chest: 40 (44, 47, 50) inches

Side to underarm: 13 (13½, 14, 14) inches

Armhole depth: 8 (8½, 9, 9) inches

Sleeve length: 17½ (18, 18½, 18½) inches

Materials
- Plymouth Galway Colornep 97 percent wool/3 percent polyester worsted weight yarn (210 yds/100g per ball): 6 (7, 8, 9) balls creme heather #501
- Size 3 (3.25mm) double-pointed and 24-inch circular needles
- Size 5 (3.75mm) straight, double-pointed and 16-inch circular needles or size needed to obtain gauge
- Cable needle
- Stitch holders
- Stitch markers
- Tapestry needle
- 2-inch clasp, Romance #901 from JHB International Inc.
- Straight pins

Gauge
17 sts and 30 rows = 4 inches/10cm in Seed st with larger needles

19 sts and 25 rows = 4 inches/10cm in St st with larger needles

To save time, take time to check gauge.

Special Abbreviation
Wrap: Sl 1 wyif, take yarn to back,

replace st on LH needle. On next row, work wrap and st it, wraps as k2tog or p2tog to maintain pat.

Pattern Notes

Seed st body begins at lower back and is worked as a rectangle to shoulders, where it is divided for fronts, which are then worked downward. Upon completion, fronts are folded under to form the unique collar and offset armhole.

Sleeve sts are picked up along this folded angle. Sleeve cap is formed with short rows and back of sleeve cap will have more sts than front. Sleeves are worked downward in St st.

Vertical body edges are finished with I-cord, while k1, p1 ribbing is used for cuffs and lower edge.

One or two clasps can be used for closure, or jacket may be left open without adornment.

Back

With larger needles, cast on 85 (93, 99, 107) sts.

Pat row (WS): K3, p1, *k1, p1, rep from * to last 3 sts, sl 3 purlwise wyif. Mark next row as RS.

Rep pat row until back measures 21 (22, 23, 23) inches, ending with a WS row.

Divide for fronts

Next row (RS): K3, work in pat across 37 (41, 43, 47) sts, sl 3 to cn and hold in front, sl 3 purlwise wyif, sl sts from cn and remaining sts to holder. (43, 47, 49, 53 right front sts)

Right Front

Work pat row across 21 (23, 24, 27) sts, wrap next st, turn, work to end of row. Work 8 pat rows even.

Rep from * to * until front measures same length as back when measured at unshaped edge. Bind off in pat.

Left Front

Sl sts from holder to LH needle. With RS facing, join yarn at center.

Next row: K3, inc (inc, dec, dec) 1 st, work in pat to last 3 sts, sl 3 purlwise wyif. (43, 47, 49, 53 left front sts)

Work left front as for right, having shaped edge at center.

Form Collar

Referring to Fig. A, fold fronts under so that shaped edges are at sides.

Try body piece on and adjust collar if necessary. Note that lowering fold of collar will also place angle of sleeve cap lower. Pin collar in place.

Measure up 11 (11½, 12, 12) inches from lower edge along each side seam and mark for underarm. Count rows of I-cord when marking for underarm to ensure both seams will be same length. Area between markers will be sleeve cap. Mark center st at point of sleeve cap. (Shown as * on Fig. B)

Sleeves

Join yarn at center marked st. With larger circular needle, pick up and k 1 st through both layers on this st only, pick up and k 1 st in each I-cord st to underarm marker, pm for seam, pull yarn across to RH marker, pick up and k 1 st in each I-cord st to center st. Remove underarm markers, leaving seam marker in place.

Shape cap

Working in St st, k center st, wrap next st, turn, p1, wrap, turn, k2, wrap, turn, p3, wrap, turn.

Continue to wrap and turn, adding 1 more st on each row until all picked-up sts on front of body have been worked.

Next row (RS): Work across all sts. Mark this row.

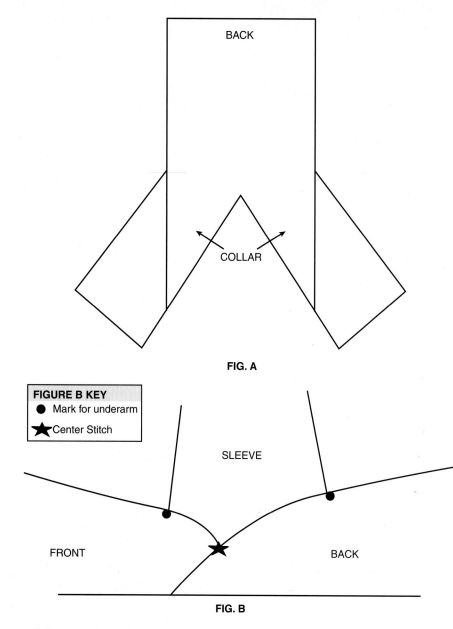

BACK

COLLAR

FIG. A

FIGURE B KEY
● Mark for underarm
★ Center Stitch

SLEEVE

FRONT

BACK

FIG. B

Working in rnds from this point, work even for 2 inches above marker.

[Dec 1 st on each side of seam marker every 12th row] 7 (7, 8, 8) times, changing to dpn as needed.

Work even until sleeve measures 15 (15½, 16, 16) inches above marked row.

Change to smaller needles and dec evenly to 44 (44, 48, 50) sts. Work even in k1, p1 rib for 2½ inches. Bind off in pat.

Lower Band

With smaller 24-inch circular needle, pick up and k 9 sts for every 10 cast-on or bound-off sts of lower edge. You must have an odd number of sts.

Next row: K3, work in k1, p1 rib to last 3 sts, sl 3 purlwise wyif.

Rep this row until ribbing measures 2 inches. Bind off in pat.

Sew clasp to front edge. ❖

City Delights Cardigan

Design by Kennita Tully

The color and design possibilities for this cardigan are endless.
Your child will love wearing it to the park or museum.

Skill Level
Intermediate***

Size
Child's 2 (4, 6, 8) Instructions
are given for smallest size, with
larger sizes in parentheses. When
only 1 number is given, it applies
to all sizes.

Finished Measurements
Chest: 14 (15, 16, 17) inches
Length: 13½ (13½, 15½, 15½) inches

Materials
- Plymouth Wildflower DK weight
  51 percent mercerized cotton/49
  percent acrylic yarn (136 yds/50g
  per ball): 5 (6, 7, 8) balls lavender
  #50 (A), 2 balls magenta #59 (B),
  1 ball bright yellow #48 (C)
- Size 5 (3.75mm) straight, and
  24-inch circular needles or size
  needed to obtain gauge
- Size 4 (3.5mm) double-pointed
  needle for tucking (1 only)
- Stitch holders
- Tapestry needle
- Crochet hook
- 3 (¾-inch) buttons

Gauge
22 sts and 40 rows = 4 inches/10cm
in garter st

To save time, take time to check
gauge.

Pattern Stitches
Cable Cast-on
*Insert RH needle between first and
2nd st on LH needle, with RH needle
pull up a st and place on LH needle.
Rep from * for needed amount of sts.

Basic Square
With B, cast on 23 sts using cable
cast-on method.

Row 1 and all WS rows: Sl 1, k to last st, p1.

Row 2: Sl 1, k9, sl 1, k2tog, psso, k9, p1.

Row 4: Sl 1, k8, sl 1, k2tog, psso, k8, p1.

Row 6: Sl 1, k7, sl 1, k2tog, psso, k7, p1.

Row 8: Sl 1, k6, sl 1, k2tog, psso, k6, p1. Change to C.

Row 10: Sl 1, k5, sl 1, k2tog, psso, k5, p1. Change to A.

Row 12: Sl 1, k4, sl 1, k2tog, psso, k4, p1.

Row 14: Sl 1, k3, sl 1, k2tog, psso, k3, p1.

Row 16: Sl 1, k2, sl 1, k2tog, psso, k2, p1.

Row 18: Sl 1, k1, sl 1, k2tog, psso, k1, p1.

Row 20: Sl 1, sl 1, k2tog, psso, p1.

Row 22: Sl 1, k2tog, psso.

Pull yarn through last st to complete square.

Pattern Notes

Sweater body is knit in 2 pieces, then joined at the back.

Modular squares are knit on and joined as knit.

Top corner square is reversed on center fronts to fold back for collar. (see Fig. 1)

Fig. 1 also shows placement of squares for front and neck borders.

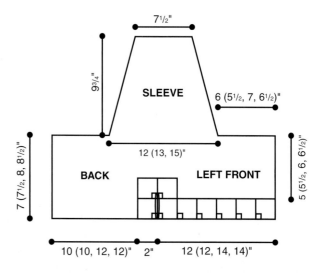

Right Body

Beg at left front with A, cast on 56 (56, 67, 67) sts. Work in garter st for 2 inches. Cut yarn and place sts on holder.

Beg at center back with A, cast on 56 (56, 67, 67) sts. Work in garter st for 4 inches, ending with a WS row.

Join front & back

Next row (RS): K back sts, cast on 22 sts at end of row using cable cast-on method, knit across front sts from holder. (134, 134, 156, 156 sts)

Work even until piece measures 7 (7½, 8, 8½) inches above center back cast-on sts.

Sleeves

Bind off 34 (31, 39, 36) sts at beg of next 2 rows. (66, 72, 78, 84 sts)

[Dec 1 st each side every 8 (8, 6, 6) rows] 12 (2, 11, 5) times, then [every 0 (6, 4, 4) rows] 0 (13, 7, 16) times. (42 sts)

Work even until sleeve measures 9¾ inches.

Bind off.

Cuff

Cable cast on 21 sts. Work Basic Square skipping first 2 rows of pat.

Add next square

Cable cast on 11 sts, with WS facing pick up and k 10 sts along right edge of first square and complete square. Add 2 more squares.

Sew to lower sleeve.

Left Body

Work as for right body, reversing shaping.

Sew pieces tog along center back.

Right Front Border

Cable cast on 12 sts, pick up and k 11 sts along front edge beg with bottom st. Complete square.

To add next square vertically, pick up 11 sts along top of square, 1 st for center st from corner of last square, and 11 sts along center front. (5, 5, 6, 6 vertical squares)

Left Front Border

Counting up from the bottom of the center front, pick up 11 sts and work down, cable cast on 12 sts and work 1 square.

To add the next square vertically, pick up and knit next 11 sts from

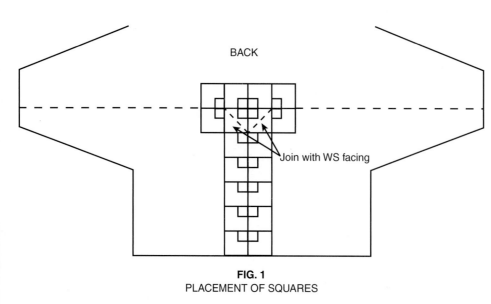

FIG. 1
PLACEMENT OF SQUARES

BACK

Join with WS facing

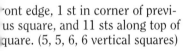

ront edge, 1 st in corner of previ-
us square, and 11 sts along top of
quare. (5, 5, 6, 6 vertical squares)

ight Back Neck Border

ick up and k 11 sts along right
eck edge, 1 st in corner for cen-
er st, and 11 sts along neckline.
omplete square.

o add next square, pick up and k 11
ts from right edge of square, 1 st for
enter, and 11 sts along neckline.

eft Back Neck Border

ick up 11 sts from neckline corner,
st in corner st for center st, and
1 sts along left side of neckline.
omplete square.

o add next square, pick up and k last
1 sts along neckline, 1 st for center
nd 11 sts from left side of square.

ront Neck Borders

/ork front neck squares as for
ack, picking up sts from WS for
p corner square.

/hen all squares are completed, sew
noulder seams joining end squares
rrough color B only.

ew side and sleeve seams.

ottom Tucked Edging

/ith RS facing and B, pick up and

k 38 (41, 44, 47) sts along lower
left front edge, 76 (82, 88, 94) sts
along back, and 38 (41, 44, 47) sts
along lower right front. (152, 164,
176, 188 sts)

*Work 8 rows in St st.

Tuck row: Pick up purl bumps
from first row and place on dpn
(approximately 20 sts at a time).
K2tog, by knitting 1 st from circular
needle with 1 st from dpn tog to
create a tuck. Continue in this
manner across row.

Purl 1 row*.

Rep from * to * once with C, then
again with A. (3 tucked color bands)

Bind off all sts.

Left Front Tucked Edging

Beg with 2nd square from top and,
pick up and k 56 (56, 67, 67) sts
along front edge.

Work in St st for 6 rows, work tuck

row and bound-off row at the same
time by working [k2tog] twice, *bind
off 1 st, k2tog. Rep from * until all
sts are bound off.

Right Front Tucked Edging

Buttonholes are made by skipping 3
sts to leave a space and casting on in
their place as follows: Pick up and k
7 (7, 18, 18) sts, *skip 3 sts and cable
cast on 3 sts, k19, rep from *, ending
with k2.

Complete band as for left front.

Finishing

Work 1 row of single crochet edging
along cuffs and collar.

Referring to photo, turn top blocks
back at an angle and tack point
in place.

Sew on buttons to correspond to
buttonholes.

Press tuck edgings from WS. ❖

Special Thanks

We would like to thank Plymouth Yarn Company for providing all the yarn used in this book. We also appreciate the help provided by Uyvonne Bingham and the Plymouth staff throughout the publishing process. It's been great working with them. We also thank the talented knitting designers whose work is featured in this collection.

Dixie Butler
Mountain Climber
Pullover, 88

Edie Eckman
Sand & Waves, 70
Top-Down Pullover, 20

Joyce Englund
Rose Tweed Cardigan, 130

Nazanin S. Fard
Country Fiesta, 24
Point-to-Point Blouse, 27
Side-to-Side Lace Sweater, 126

Lynnette Harter
City Sidewalks, 144

Katharine Hunt
Cuff-to-Cuff Kid, 44
Indigo Cotton Vest, 8

Joan McGowan-Michael
Night on the Town, 156

Kathy Sasser
Adirondack Weekend, 100
Halloween Fun Sweater, 35

Mary J. Saunders
Cable & Bobbles Vest, 152

E. J. Slayton
Chevron Lace Top, 66
Lace Scallops Vest, 148

Ann E. Smith
A Touch of Norway, 134

Kennita Tully
Blue Jeans Beach Vest, 54
City Delights Cardigan, 172
Crescent Band Cardigan, 140
Pair of Sailing Pullovers, 82

Panels in Plum Pullover, 122

Barbara Venishnick
City Evening Jacket, 164
Contrapposto Symphony
Sweater, 160
Homage to Horst, 94
Periwinkle Panels, 30
Royal Ashanti Jacket, 16
Rustic Cables, 77

Lois S. Young
Beachcomber Pullover, 74
Mountain Greenery, 118
Summer Swing Top, 50

Diane Zangl
Amigo Top, 62
Camp Cables, 91
Caravan Vest, 12
Downtown Excursion Jacket, 168
Summer Tea Top, 58